GREAT
TED
TALKS
CREATIVITY

D0877775

Portable Press

An imprint of Printers Row Publishing Group
10350 Barnes Canyon Road, Suite 100, San Diego, CA 92121
www.portablepress.com • mail@portablepress.com

Printers Row Publishing Group is a division of Readerlink Distribution Services, LLC.
Portable Press is a registered trademark of Readerlink Distribution Services, LLC.

Correspondence regarding the content of this book should be sent to Portable
Press, Editorial Department, at the above address. Author and illustration inquiries
should be sent to Quarto Publishing Plc, 6 Blundell St, London N7 9BH,
www.quartoknows.com.

Portable Press
Publisher: Peter Norton • Associate Publisher: Ana Parker
Editor: Dan Mansfield
Senior Product Manager: Kathryn C. Dalby

Produced by Quarto Publishing plc
Publisher: Mark Searle
Creative Director: James Evans
Art Director: Katherine Radcliffe
Commissioning Editor: Sorrel Wood
Managing Editors: Isheeta Mustafi and Jacqui Sayers
In-house Editor: Abbie Sharman
Editor: David Price-Goodfellow • Designer: Tony Seddon

Library of Congress Control Number: 2019950987
ISBN: 978-1-64517-215-4

Printed in China

24 23 22 21 20   1 2 3 4 5

GREAT TED TALKS

CREATIVITY

An Unofficial Guide with Words of Wisdom from 100 TED Speakers

TOM MAY

PORTABLE PRESS

San Diego, California

CONTENTS

INTRODUCTION

If you've ever watched a good TED talk, you'll know that it's a surefire way to feel invigorated, energized, and inspired. In fact, you probably keep telling yourself you should watch more.

In truth, however, it's not practical for most of us to sit down and plow through the thousands of hours of TED talks that are available to watch free online. That's where this book comes in. It aims to serve as a taster menu, introducing you to the best TED talks for creatives, as well as sharing some of the speakers' keenest insights in nontechnical words that everyone can understand.

Over the following pages, the very best advice from TED speakers—both in the creative industries and beyond—has been distilled into bite-sized chunks that you can start following today. The aim is to help boost your creativity, give you fresh ideas, and progress your career, without you having to watch each talk from start to finish. That said, if a particular piece of advice really resonates with you, you may want to do just that, and so we explain on the opposite page how to watch the talks online for free.

Some of the talks featured in this book focus on specific professions, such as painting, graphic design, or poetry. But most of them cover much broader themes: tips and ideas that can be applied to *any* creative endeavor, whether that be art, sculpture, illustration, design, animation, writing, music, filmmaking, acting—or indeed any task where imagination, creativity, and "thinking outside the box" are crucial.

In short, this book is packed with life lessons and practical tips, allowing you to take your skills and creativity to the next level whatever your chosen discipline.

How to Use This Book

This book of tips is designed to be quick and easy to peruse. You can read it from front to back or back to front, or dip in and out whenever you need inspiration—it's completely up to you. And if you want to refer back to a tip later but can't remember where it is, that's no problem. At the back of the book are two indexes—one for topics, and one for the speakers quoted—so it's always easy to find what you're looking for.

Crucially, you don't need to have seen a single TED talk to enjoy this book. But maybe you'd like to deepen your learning and watch one of the talks now? Again, that's no problem, as at the time of publication, all of the talks are available to watch free online.

You will find the links to the talks included in this book as part of the speaker index. Or you can simply go to ted.com, click on the magnifying glass in the right-hand corner, and type in the title of the talk. For example, to find the first talk mentioned in the book (on page 10), you'd type "Creativity and Play."

Occasionally, though, a talk might not be there. During the production of this book, a few of them hadn't yet made it onto the TED website. But don't worry: they're all available to view on YouTube too. In other words, if a talk doesn't come up when you type it into TED.com, go to YouTube.com and search there instead. In this case, be sure to put the title in quote marks (" ") so that YouTube knows exactly what it's looking for (there are a few billion other videos on the site, so it pays to be specific).

Alternatively, you might prefer to type the title into Google (again, surrounded by quote marks). In that case, the talk should appear in Google's listings under the "Videos" heading.

Whether you choose simply to read the book or use it as a stepping-stone to the wider universe of watching TED talks, it's time to open your mind and be inspired creatively. Prepare to get a whole new perspective on your hobby or profession and where it can take you!

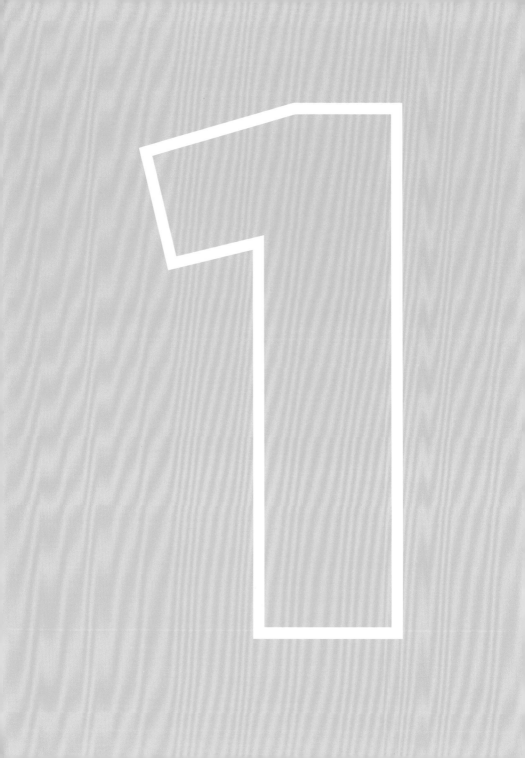

BE OPEN to new ways of thinking

The first step to becoming more creative is to open yourself up to new ways of thinking and perceiving the world.

THINK LIKE A CHILD

Stop being so "adult" and let your imagination fly.

Want to be more creative? Then you need to think like a child. Tim Brown, the chair of the design firm IDEO, offers a simple example of how to do this in practice.

In his talk "Creativity and Play," Brown asks the members of the audience to take a piece of paper and draw the person sitting next to them in thirty seconds flat. Cue lots of laughter and embarrassment about how bad the sketches are. "I think I'm hearing a few 'sorrys'!" Brown notes. "Yup, that's exactly what happens every time you do this with adults."

And here lies the rub. "If you try the same exercise with kids, they have no embarrassment at all," Brown points out. "They just quite happily show their masterpiece to whoever wants to look at it. But as they learn to become adults, they become much more sensitive to the opinions of others, and they lose that sense of freedom."

In short, to come up with inventive and creative ideas, you need to free your mind from the judgment of others—just like kids do. And one way to do that in practice, says Brown, is by turning creative tasks into a form of organized play.

Taking the sketching task as an example, Brown says, "Imagine if you did the same task with friends while you were drinking in a pub. But everybody agreed to play a game where the worst sketch artist bought the next round of drinks. That framework of rules would have turned an embarrassing, difficult situation into a fun game. As a result, we'd all feel perfectly secure."

In other words, by finding ways to turn our creative work into play, we can tap into our inner child and unleash our imaginations, just as we did when we were kids.

Q FIND OUT MORE

Tim Brown's talk:
"Creativity and Play"
2008

Also try Harun Robert's talk:
"Think Like a Child!"
2014

IF YOU TRY THE SAME EXERCISE WITH KIDS, THEY HAVE NO EMBARRASSMENT AT ALL.
TIM BROWN

TAKE THE THIRTY-DAY CHALLENGE

Use this great idea to shake off your creative cobwebs.

Is there something you've always wanted to do, but just haven't? In his talk, Matt Cutts suggests that you try it for thirty days.

Cutts, an engineer at Google, describes a time when he was feeling stuck in a rut and so did just that. He began with quite a simple challenge—taking a photo every day for a month—but says it made a big impact on his life.

"It turns out thirty days is just about the right amount of time to add a new habit or subtract a habit—like watching the news—from your life," he explains. "Instead of the months flying by, forgotten, the time was much more memorable. I remember exactly where I was, and what I was doing [each] day. I also noticed that as I started to do more and harder thirty-day challenges, my self-confidence grew. I went from a desk-dwelling computer nerd to the kind of guy who bikes to work—for fun!"

Ultimately, Cutts ended up hiking to the top of Mount Kilimanjaro and writing a novel, two things he'd never thought about doing before. And the lesson he learned was that you can do anything for thirty days if you want it badly enough.

"What are you waiting for?" Cutts concludes. "I guarantee you, the next thirty days are going to pass whether you like it or not. So, why not think about something you've always wanted to try and give it a shot, for the next thirty days?"

> **THINK ABOUT SOMETHING YOU HAVE ALWAYS WANTED TO TRY AND GIVE IT A SHOT.**
> MATT CUTTS

Q FIND OUT MORE

Matt Cutts's talk:
"Try Something New for Thirty Days"
2011

Also try Emma Van Der Merwe's talk:
"Why I Do Something Everyday that Scares Me"
2016

DO LOTS OF THINGS AT ONCE

Multitasking actually makes you more creative.

If you want to succeed at a task, you might plan to focus on it solely, to the exclusion of everything else. But according to author Tim Harford, you'd be wrong to do so. In fact, as he reveals in his talk "A Powerful Way to Unleash Your Natural Creativity," multitasking will actually make you more creative and productive.

The world's most enduringly creative people, Harford notes, tend to juggle multiple projects and move between them as the mood strikes. Personalities as diverse as Albert Einstein, Charles Darwin, Twyla Tharp, and Michael Crichton have found their inspiration and productivity in this way, and Harford believes that's no accident.

"Creativity often comes when you take an idea from its original context and you move it somewhere else," he reasons. "It's easier to think outside the box if you spend your time clambering from one box into another."

The way to make multitasking work, Harford stresses, is to do it slowly, not frantically. "We're used to lapsing into multitasking out of desperation. We're in a hurry; we want to do everything at once. [But] if we were willing to slow multitasking down, we might find that it works quite brilliantly."

He compares this to "working on a crossword puzzle and you can't figure out the answer . . . because the wrong answer is stuck in your head." The solution is often to "switch topics, switch context; you'll forget the wrong answer, and that gives the right answer space to pop into your mind."

Q FIND OUT MORE

Tim Harford's talk:
"A Powerful Way to Unleash Your Natural Creativity"
2018

Also try Dave Cornthwaite's talk:
"Do Something New Every Single Day"
2014

WALK THROUGH AN IDEA

Moving your feet boosts your brainpower.

When we're struggling to find a way forward on a creative task, it's often tempting to go for a walk to shake off the cobwebs. Often, though, we'll resist that urge and tell ourselves we should instead "knuckle down" and work on the problem "properly."

According to behavioral and learning scientist Marily Oppezzo, however, you're better off with the first option. Because going for a walk—whether that's a stroll outside or a stint on a treadmill indoors—really *does* help you become more creative.

In her talk "Want to Be More Creative? Go for a Walk," Oppezzo relates how she ran four studies with a variety of people. She asked participants to think of as many alternative ways as possible to use everyday objects—for example, "What else would you do with a key?"

Oppezzo found that those who spent time *sitting down* before the test produced twenty ideas per person on average. But those who spent time *walking* before the test came up with almost twice as many.

There was also an interesting difference between the members of one particular group—who walked, then sat for a while, and then took the test—and those of another group, who went for a walk and then took the test straight away. The latter did significantly better than the former. "So, the implication of this," concludes Oppezzo, "is that you should go for a walk before your next big meeting and just start brainstorming right away."

Q FIND OUT MORE

Marily Oppezzo's talk:
"Want to Be More Creative? Go for a Walk"
2017

. . . .

Also try Wendy Suzuki's talk:
"The Brain-changing Benefits of Exercise"
2017

TURN PROCRASTINATION INTO A POSITIVE

Putting things off can actually be good.

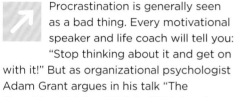

Procrastination is generally seen as a bad thing. Every motivational speaker and life coach will tell you: "Stop thinking about it and get on with it!" But as organizational psychologist Adam Grant argues in his talk "The Surprising Habits of Original Thinkers," a little bit of procrastination can actually make you more creative.

"Take Leonardo da Vinci," he points out. "He toiled on and off for sixteen years on the *Mona Lisa*. He felt like a failure. He wrote as much in his journal. But some of the diversions he took in optics transformed the way that he modeled light and made him into a much better painter."

Grant also offers the example of Martin Luther King Jr. "The night before the biggest speech of his life, the March on Washington, he was up past 3:00 a.m., rewriting it," he explains. "He's sitting in the audience waiting for his turn to go on stage, and he is still scribbling notes and crossing out lines. When he gets on stage, eleven minutes in, he leaves his prepared remarks to utter four words that changed the course of history: 'I have a dream.' That was not in the script."

In short, by putting things off until the last possible minute, procrastinating can sometimes lead to exceptional results. It's not about being lazy. As Hollywood screenwriter and director Aaron Sorkin once put it, "You call it procrastinating, I call it thinking." For more on working at a slower pace, turn to page 168.

🔍 FIND OUT MORE

**Adam Grant's talk:
"The Surprising Habits of Original Thinkers"
2016**

. . . .

**Also try Tim Urban's talk:
"Inside the Mind of a Master Procrastinator"
2016**

TAKE LEONARDO DA VINCI. HE TOILED ON AND OFF FOR SIXTEEN YEARS ON THE *MONA LISA*. HE FELT LIKE A FAILURE.

ADAM GRANT

MAKE USELESS THINGS

Turn off the negative voices in your head and start having fun.

Being creative is all about coming up with new ideas. But if you try to work conventionally, that can often be difficult, as your brain defaults to all the well-worn pathways that drive you toward predictable and unoriginal thinking.

Therefore, it can sometimes be good to mix things up and do them a little differently. Simone Giertz suggests one approach you could take in her talk "Why You Should Make Useless Things." That's literally what she has been doing: making wacky devices. Her inventions—which are designed to chop vegetables, cut hair, apply lipstick, and more—rarely succeed, but that's kind of the point. From a helmet that brushes your teeth for you, to a machine that hands you a glass of water, it's all about unleashing your imagination and seeing where it takes you.

"The true beauty of making useless things [is] this acknowledgment that you don't always know what the best answer is," Giertz says. "It turns off that voice in your head that tells you that you know exactly how the world works. Maybe a toothbrush helmet isn't the answer, but at least you're asking the question." And who knows, in the long term, what you might end up creating as a result?

Discover more about seeing the world in a different way on page 62.

Q FIND OUT MORE

Learn more in Simone Giertz's talk: "Why You Should Make Useless Things"
2018

Also try Chris Griffiths's talk: "Think Different"
2017

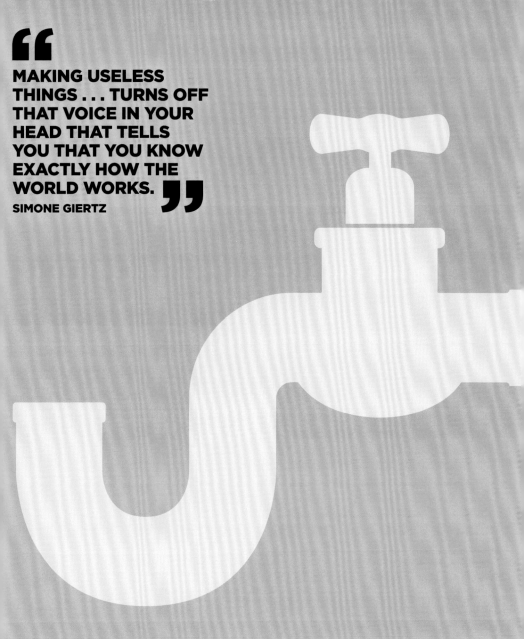

MAKING USELESS THINGS . . . TURNS OFF THAT VOICE IN YOUR HEAD THAT TELLS YOU THAT YOU KNOW EXACTLY HOW THE WORLD WORKS.

SIMONE GIERTZ

LISTEN TO YOUNGER PEOPLE

It's not just the old who can teach the young.

Encountering different perspectives is a great way to stimulate new creative ideas. And one of the easiest ways to do this is to tap into people from different generations.

In his talk "What Baby Boomers Can Learn from Millennials at Work—and Vice Versa," Chip Conley argues that age diversity makes companies stronger, but only if there's a culture that encourages each generation to learn from the others. In reality, though, "We often don't trust each other enough to actually share our respective wisdom." And that's partly because we're still stuck in the mind-set that the old teach and the young learn.

Instead, Conley says, in a world where the most innovative companies are led by the young, the relationship needs to go both ways. "The modern elder is as much an intern as . . . a mentor," he says. "They realize, in a world that is changing so quickly, [a millennial's] beginner's mind and their catalytic curiosity is a life-affirming elixir, not just for themselves but for everyone around them."

What Conley calls "intergenerational improv" has long been standard practice among musicians. "Think Tony Bennett and Lady Gaga, or Wynton Marsalis and the Young Stars of Jazz," he points out. So whatever your discipline, ask yourself whether "mutual mentorship" might also make you better and more creative.

Q FIND OUT MORE

Chip Conley's talk:
"What Baby Boomers Can Learn from Millennials at Work—and Vice Versa"
2018

Also try Adora Svitak's talk:
"What Adults Can Learn from Kids"
2010

> **WE OFTEN DON'T TRUST EACH OTHER ENOUGH TO ACTUALLY SHARE OUR RESPECTIVE WISDOM.**
>
> **CHIP CONLEY**

REMIX OTHER PEOPLE'S IDEAS

Combine established ideas to make something new.

When we set out to be creative, we obviously want our work to be original. But that doesn't mean we can't be inspired by others. In fact, one of the best ways of creating something amazing can be to take other people's ideas and "remix" them into something new.

As Kirby Ferguson explains in his talk "Embrace the Remix," this is a well-established approach. He reminds us of Henry Ford's famous quote, "I invented nothing new; I simply assembled the discoveries of other men, behind whom were centuries of work," as well as Pablo Picasso's pithier line, "Good artists copy. Great artists steal."

For a more recent example, Ferguson points to Bob Dylan. "Like all folk singers, he copied melodies, he transformed them, he combined them with new lyrics which were frequently their own concoction of previous stuff," he says. Steve Jobs acted similarly, "remixing" existing technologies to create the all-conquering iPhone.

In summary, our most celebrated creators borrow, steal, and transform, so don't be afraid of doing so yourself. "Our creativity comes from without, not from within," Ferguson argues. "We are not self-made. We are dependent on one another, and admitting this to ourselves isn't an embrace of mediocrity and derivativeness: it's a liberation from our misconceptions." Learn more about remixing on page 72.

> **OUR CREATIVITY COMES FROM WITHOUT, NOT FROM WITHIN: WE ARE NOT SELF-MADE.**
> **KIRBY FERGUSON**

Q FIND OUT MORE

Kirby Ferguson's talk:
"Embrace the Remix"
2012

Also try Golan Levin's talk:
"Art that Looks Back at You"
2019

GUIDED MASTERY

Overcome your fears, step by step.

So far, we've focused on ways to come up with creative ideas. However, what if you do have ideas but don't have confidence in them? In his talk "How to Build Your Creative Confidence," David Kelley, founder of the design firm IDEO, explains how you can boost your confidence through "guided mastery." The term was coined by psychologist Albert Bandura, who cured people's fear of snakes through a gradual step-by-step process.

"He'd take people to this two-way mirror looking into the room where the snake was," explains Kelley. "He'd get them comfortable with that. Then, through a series of steps, he'd move them and they'd be standing in the doorway with the door open, and they'd be looking in there. And he'd get them comfortable with that . . . They'd eventually touch the snake."

Lack of confidence is essentially a fear of failure. So when you face that fear—step by step, as with the snake—you'll soon find it ebbing and disappearing. Kelley has adapted the process for Stanford University's Hasso Plattner Institute of Design, aka the d.school, and it's helped many people realize they can be more creative than they thought possible.

"People from all different kinds of disciplines, they think of themselves as only analytical," he explains. "And they come in and they go through the process . . . they build confidence and now they think of themselves differently. And they're totally emotionally excited about the fact that they walk around thinking of themselves as a creative person."

Q FIND OUT MORE

David Kelley's talk:
"How to Build Your Creative Confidence"
2012

Also try Tim Ferriss's talk:
"Why You Should Define Your Fears Instead of Your Goals"
2017

DEFY CONVENTIONAL WISDOM

Don't like the way things are done? Shake them up!

> ❝ **HOW MUCH OF THAT CONVENTIONAL WISDOM IS ALL CONVENTION AND NO WISDOM?** ❞
> **FRANKLIN LEONARD**

Are you "playing the game" but getting nowhere? Then maybe you should change the rules of that game. That's what Franklin Leonard did, as he recalls in his talk "How I Accidentally Changed the Way Movies Get Made."

In 2005 Leonard was working for Leonardo DiCaprio's production company Appian Way, where one of his tasks was to read and judge scripts. "Fundamentally, it's triage," he explains. "And when you're in triage, you tend to default to conventional wisdom about 'what works' and what doesn't."

Despite this, he sensed somehow that the "conventional wisdom" wasn't correct, and that great scripts—such as those focused on women or people of color— were getting missed as a result. Instead, he e-mailed seventy-five industry people and asked them to send in the unmade scripts they'd truly loved.

Leonard compiled the results in a spreadsheet, called it the "Black List," and e-mailed it back to the same folks. Soon—to his surprise—the list was being shared around the industry and creating an enormous buzz.

Six months later, an agent pitched a script to him and said, "I have it on really good authority this is going to be the number one script on next year's Black List!" Leonard was dumbfounded. The

agent clearly had no idea where the Black List had originated, and the document seemed to have taken on a life of its own.

Leonard decided there and then to compile another Black List, and it's since become an annual event, with scripts like *Juno*, *Slumdog Millionaire*, and *Little Miss Sunshine* all getting the green light as a result.

The moral? "As a rule, we tend to default to conventional wisdom," says Leonard. "And I think it's important that we ask ourselves, constantly, how much of that conventional wisdom is all convention and no wisdom? And at what cost?"

Q FIND OUT MORE

Franklin Leonard's talk: "How I Accidentally Changed the Way Movies Get Made" 2018

Also try Doug Burgum's talk: "Transcending Conventional Wisdom with Courageous Curiosity" 2012

TALK TO YOUR SELF-DOUBT

Beat creative block by having a conversation with thin air.

> **HE JUST LOOKED UP AT THE SKY, AND HE SAID, 'EXCUSE ME, CAN YOU NOT SEE THAT I'M DRIVING?'**
> **ELIZABETH GILBERT**

All creatives struggle with self-doubt. But here's a trick that Elizabeth Gilbert, the author of *Eat, Pray, Love*, learned from legendary musician Tom Waits.

As Gilbert recalls in her talk "Your Elusive Creative Genius," one day Waits was driving down the freeway and a fragment of melody appeared in his head. But because he was unable to write it down there and then, he started fretting about forgetting it forever.

As a result, all the old anxieties and self-doubt that had tortured Waits throughout his career began to bubble up. Then, however, he did something unexpected. "He just looked up at the sky, and he said, 'Excuse me, can you not see that I'm driving? Do I look like I can write down a song right now? If you really want to exist, come back at a more opportune moment when I can take care of you. Otherwise, go bother somebody else today. Go bother Leonard Cohen.'"

Years later, Gilbert fell into a "pit of despair" herself, fearing her follow-up to *Eat, Pray, Love* was turning into "the worst book ever written." So she tried Waits's

trick, and it worked. The book, *Committed*, ultimately spent fifty-seven weeks at number one on the *New York Times* best-seller list.

So, next time you're feeling unsure of yourself, try talking to the open air: vent your frustrations and challenge your self-doubt out loud. It might seem silly, but it really does work.

🔍 FIND OUT MORE

Elizabeth Gilbert's talk:
"Your Elusive Creative Genius"
2009

Also try Melissa Root's talk:
"Eliminate Self-Doubt: Tap Your Root Response"
2017

BE SMART and find inspiration in unusual places

We're all seeking creative inspiration, so if you look in the obvious places, you'll just end up thinking like everybody else. This chapter reveals how successful people have found inspiration in the most unlikely places.

READ THE OBITUARIES

In death, we find some of the most positive stories in life.

Looking for new sources of inspiration? Then read the daily obituaries—they're overflowing with it.

Entrepreneur Lux Narayan does just that, starting his day with scrambled eggs and the question "Who died today, and why?" He feels this provides a great balance to the overall sense of negativity we get from the news in general.

"If you think about it, the front page of the newspaper is usually bad news, and cues man's failures," he explains in his talk "What I Learned from 2,000 Obituaries." In stark contrast, "an instance where bad news cues accomplishment is at the end of the paper, in the obituaries."

By analyzing twenty months' worth of obituaries, Narayan discovered that humanity is capable of more incredible feats than we often hear about.

"The overwhelming majority of obituaries featured people famous and non-famous, who did seemingly extraordinary things," he notes. "They made a positive dent in the fabric of life. They helped."

And the lesson for the rest of us? "Ask yourselves as you go back to your daily lives, 'How am I using my talents to help society?' Because the most powerful lesson here is, if more people lived their lives trying to be famous in death, the world would be a much better place."

Q FIND OUT MORE

Lux Narayan's talk:
"What I Learned from 2,000 Obituaries"
2017

. . . .

Also try Minke Haveman's talk:
"The Importance of Leaving a Legacy"
2015

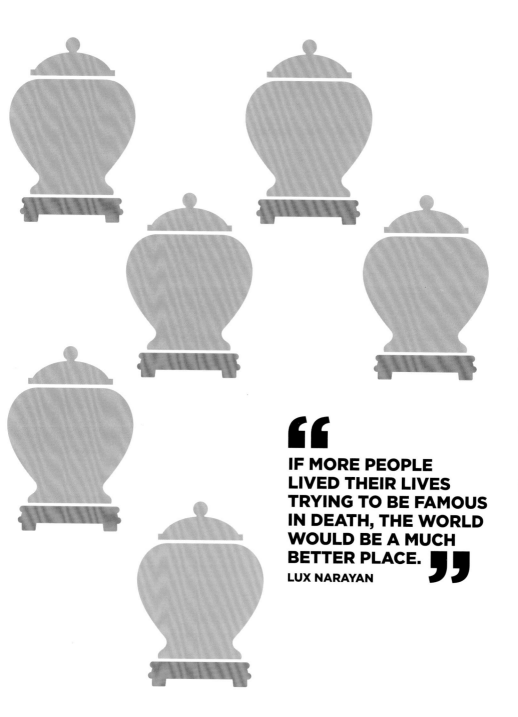

"

**IF MORE PEOPLE
LIVED THEIR LIVES
TRYING TO BE FAMOUS
IN DEATH, THE WORLD
WOULD BE A MUCH
BETTER PLACE.** **"**

LUX NARAYAN

13/100
ASK A BARTENDER

A nonexpert can often be the best person to help with a breakthrough.

One of the best ways to get a fresh perspective on a problem can be to ask someone who's completely uninvolved in it. Tech entrepreneur Eric Berridge gives a great example of this in his talk "Why Tech Needs the Humanities."

Berridge was at a software company of 200 people that was about to go out of business because it simply couldn't please a client. And so his team went to the bar to drown their sorrows.

"We're hanging out with our bartender friend Jeff," Berridge recalls, "and he's doing what all good bartenders do. He's commiserating with us, making us feel better, relating to our pain, saying, 'Hey, these guys are overblowing it. Don't worry about it.' And finally, he deadpans us and says, 'Why don't you send me in there? I can figure it out.'"

Jeff was no programmer; in fact, he was a philosophy college dropout. But with nothing to lose, Berridge's team took him up on his offer. And incredibly, it worked.

"He had completely disarmed their fixation on the programming skill," enthuses Berridge. "He had changed the conversation, even changing what we were building. The conversation was now about what we were going to build and why. And . . . the client became one of our best references."

So, the next time you have a problem, consider asking someone with no skin in the game and no expertise in the area. He or she may well have the answers you've been looking for.

🔍 FIND OUT MORE

Eric Berridge's talk:
"Why Tech Needs the Humanities"
2017

. . . .

Also try Giovanni Corazza's talk:
"Creative Thinking—How to Get Out of the Box and Generate Ideas"
2014

INVENT NEW WORDS

Get your creative juices flowing by adding to an imaginary dictionary.

Words are an essential tool for communicating our creative ideas. But there are still many emotions, feelings, and phenomena for which no words exist—and so John Koenig likes to invent new ones.

Author of *The Dictionary of Obscure Sorrows*, Koenig's on a mission to find holes in the language of emotion and to try to fill them. As he puts it, "We have a way of talking about all those human peccadilloes and quirks of the human condition that we all feel, but may not think to talk about, because we don't have the words to do it." Two examples of his new words are "*jouska*, which is the kind of hypothetical conversation that you compulsively play out in your head," and "*zielschmerz*, which is the dread of getting what you want."

Koenig encourages you to do the same, and believes it can really help you feel empowered. Because once you start forming new words, "you realize . . . this world was built by people no smarter than you. Then you can reach out and touch those walls, and even put your hand through them and realize that you have the power to change it."

Why not give it a try? Think of something that has no word to describe it, then make one up. Use it in conversation and see if people start adopting it themselves. It's a heap of fun!

> **YOU CAN REACH OUT AND TOUCH THOSE WALLS, AND EVEN PUT YOUR HAND THROUGH THEM AND REALIZE THAT YOU HAVE THE POWER TO CHANGE [THIS WORLD].**
> **JOHN KOENIG**

Q FIND OUT MORE

John Koenig's talk:
"Beautiful New Words to Describe Obscure Emotions"
2016
....
Also try Erin McKean's talk:
"Go Ahead, Make Up New Words!"
2014

USE THE WRONG TOOLS

Finding ways to work with the wrong equipment can be a boost to your creativity.

A bad workman, as the saying goes, blames his tools. But you can extend this idea even further and say that using the wrong tools can actually be a good thing.

As Tim Harford points out in his talk "How Frustration Can Make Us More Creative," a little mess can often lead to surprising and exceptional work. He gives the example of a concert by the American jazz musician Keith Jarrett at the Cologne Opera in 1975. It almost didn't happen, because the venue had provided the wrong piano.

"This one had this harsh, tinny upper register, because all the felt had worn away," explains Harford. "The black notes were sticking, the white notes were out of tune, the pedals didn't work, and the piano itself was just too small."

Unfortunately, the organizer couldn't arrange a replacement in time, and although Jarrett had initially refused to play, he ultimately felt sorry for her and agreed to give the concert. Then something unexpected happened.

"Within moments, it became clear that something magical was happening," explains Harford. "Jarrett was avoiding those upper registers. He was sticking to the middle tones of the keyboard, which gave the piece a soothing, ambient quality. But also, because the piano was so quiet, he had to set up these rumbling, repetitive

WITHIN MOMENTS, IT BECAME CLEAR THAT SOMETHING MAGICAL WAS HAPPENING.

TIM HARFORD

riffs in the bass. And he stood up, twisting, pounding down on the keys, desperately trying to create enough volume to reach the people in the back row."

In short, by using an "unplayable" piano, the artist ended up giving an electrifying and magical performance. "The recording of the Cologne concert is the best-selling piano album in history and the best-selling solo jazz album in history," notes Harford. Which makes you wonder, what amazing things could we all create if we sometimes use the "wrong" tools?

🔍 **FIND OUT MORE**

Tim Harford's talk:
"How Frustration Can Make Us More Creative"
2015

. . . .

Also try Navi Radjou's talk:
"Creative Problem-solving in the Face of Extreme Limits"
2014

BREAK FROM THE NORM

Doing something in a new way can change your whole perspective.

In the previous example, jazz musician Keith Jarrett had to cope with playing the wrong type of piano. But what if there had been no piano at all? The equivalent happened to American artist Janet Echelman when her paints went missing, and how she responded can serve as an inspiration to us all.

In readiness for an exhibition of her paintings in India, Echelman shipped her paints and traveled to Mahabalipuram, but the paints didn't arrive. So she decided to improvise. "This fishing village was famous for sculpture," she recalls. "But to make large forms was too heavy and expensive. I went for a walk on the beach, watching the fishermen bundle their nets into mounds on the sand. I'd seen it every day, but this time I saw it differently: a new approach to sculpture, a way to make volumetric form without heavy solid materials."

Echelman started to collaborate with the fishermen, using their nets to create her first project, a self-portrait. "We hoisted them on poles to photograph," she explains. "I discovered their soft surfaces revealed every ripple of wind in constantly changing patterns. I was mesmerized."

She continued studying craft traditions and collaborating with artisans around the world. It took her art in a whole new direction, one that has made her famous worldwide. And the lesson? Most creative people aren't good at just one thing, and experimenting and improvising in the face of adversity can turn challenges into new and exciting opportunities.

FIND OUT MORE

Janet Echelman's talk: "Taking Imagination Seriously" 2011

Also try David Schneider's talk: "A Different Perspective Can Change Everything" 2017

**THIS TIME I SAW
IT DIFFERENTLY:
A NEW APPROACH
TO SCULPTURE.**
JANET ECHELMAN

17/100

SEE THE BEAUTY IN EVERYDAY LIFE

Inspiration is everywhere around us, if only we look for it.

When we're looking for creative inspiration, we might visit an art gallery to view work by history's greatest painters, or listen to music by its greatest composers. But we don't have to make a special effort to discover beauty: it's all around us, in day-to-day places and situations.

In her talk "The Unexpected Beauty of Everyday Sounds," Meklit Hadero explains how ambient sounds—from birdsong and the tones of human language to the sound of our own heartbeats—can inspire any songwriter.

She gives the example of her favorite Ethiopian word, *indey*, which means "No!" or "How could he?" "It has a pitch, it has a melody," she says. "You can almost see the shape as it springs from someone's mouth. *In-dey*: it dips, and then raises again." It's a similar case with *lickih nehu*, which means "it is correct." "What I did was, I took the melody and the phrasing of those words and phrases, and I turned them into musical parts to use in these short compositions. And I like to write bass lines, so they both ended up kind of as bass lines."

Of course, the same point also applies to visual media. Aesthetic inspiration is everywhere around us, from the natural world to man-made objects—we just have to teach our minds to take it all in.

In short, wherever you are, open your eyes and ears. Whatever your creative discipline, you won't find it difficult to find inspiration.

Q FIND OUT MORE

Meklit Hadero's talk:
"The Unexpected Beauty of Everyday Sounds"
2015
....

Also try Julian Treasure's talk:
"The 4 Ways Sound Affects Us"
2009

LEARN FROM OTHER CULTURES

It's the little differences in the way people see things that can make the most impact.

Being creative is often about seeing the world in a different way. It can therefore be useful to discover the different ways people in other countries and cultures perceive the world. That's the central topic of Derek Sivers's talk "Weird, or Just Different?," which highlights instances of how the way we see things isn't always shared by others.

For example, Japanese addresses are based on block numbers (which largely don't exist in the United States), not street names (which largely don't exist in Japan). West African musicians count their music in terms of two-three-four-one rather than one-two-three-four. And in China there are doctors whose job it is to keep you healthy, so you pay them when you're well, not when you're sick.

"I love that sometimes we need to go to the opposite side of the world to realize assumptions we didn't even know we had, and realize that the opposite of them may also be true," says Sivers. In fact, we don't even have to travel abroad: different personal perspectives can equally be observed in different regions of our own country, or even within different communities, be they religious, or related to work or hobbies.

The important thing is to keep our eyes and ears open to all those small but significant differences that can tell us so much about our own assumptions.

 FIND OUT MORE

**Derek Sivers's talk:
"Weird, or Just Different?"
2009**

**Also try Julien S. Bourrelle's talk:
"Learn a New Culture"
2017**

HOW TO GET "AHA!" MOMENTS

Create an environment where amazing ideas happen naturally.

We all dream of those "Aha!" moments, when an amazing idea hits. But what if there was a way to *make sure* they happen?

In his talk "The Search for 'Aha!' Moments," Matt Goldman—cofounder of the theater troupe Blue Man Group—asks, "Is there a way to take those 'Aha!' moments, those breakthroughs that seem to happen randomly and occasionally, and have them happen intentionally and frequently?" And his answer: It's all down to iteration—constantly working on an idea and improving it, bit by bit.

Goldman gives an example of Blue Man Group trying to illustrate the consumption-waste loop in a funny and surprising way. It didn't happen overnight, but followed months of failure. "And I can definitively tell you," he says, "that oatmeal, Jell-O, Cream of Wheat, Gak, pudding, clay, tapioca, Silly Putty, and tomato paste do not slide through a tube that's coiled up under your costumes [and] that's meant to come out an orifice in your chest and spray toward the audience. It won't happen."

Finally, after lots of experiments, their "Aha!" moment came. "Who knew that bananas would have the exact right properties to stay solid even when pushed through a tube with forced air, yet slippery enough to have the dramatic oozing effect that we were looking for?" Goldman exclaims.

The lesson? Don't wait around for big ideas to strike like a bolt from the blue. "Aha!" moments are more likely to stem from steady iteration than sudden inspiration.

🔍 FIND OUT MORE

Matt Goldman's talk:
"The Search for 'Aha!' Moments"
2017

Also try Gary Klein's talk:
"Lightbulb Moment"
2015

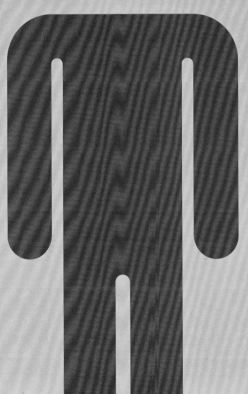

"IS THERE A WAY TO TAKE THOSE 'AHA!' MOMENTS, THOSE BREAKTHROUGHS THAT SEEM TO HAPPEN RANDOMLY AND OCCASIONALLY, AND HAVE THEM HAPPEN INTENTIONALLY AND FREQUENTLY?"

MATT GOLDMAN

FIND NEW WAYS TO SHOW YOUR ART

Moving outside the gallery can give you a fresh perspective.

> **ANYONE WHO MAKES WORK CAN SHOW IT. AROUND 300 ART INSTALLATIONS AND COUNTLESS ARTISTIC GESTURES GO TO THE PLAYA.**
> **NORA ATKINSON**

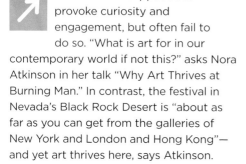 Museums are supposed to provoke curiosity and engagement, but often fail to do so. "What is art for in our contemporary world if not this?" asks Nora Atkinson in her talk "Why Art Thrives at Burning Man." In contrast, the festival in Nevada's Black Rock Desert is "about as far as you can get from the galleries of New York and London and Hong Kong"— and yet art thrives here, says Atkinson.

Why? For a start, there are no gatekeepers. "Anyone who makes work can show it," she notes. "Around 300 art installations and countless artistic gestures go to the playa [dry lake]. None of them are sold there. At the end of the week, if the works aren't burned, artists have to cart them back out and store them. It's a tremendous labor of love."

The desert itself also makes the art different. "For a work to succeed," Atkinson points out, "it has to be portable enough to make the journey, rugged enough to withstand the wind and weather and participants, stimulating in daylight and darkness, and engaging without interpretation.

"Encounters with monumental and intimate works here feel surreal. Scale has

a tendency to fool the eyes. What looked enormous in an artist's studio could get lost on the playa, but there are virtually no spatial limits, so artists can dream as big as they can build. Some pieces bowl you over by their grace and others by the sheer audacity it took to bring them here."

The moral of this story? If you want your art to be unique, perhaps you should find a unique place to exhibit it. Let that shape the creation process accordingly, and see what cool things happen.

🔍 FIND OUT MORE

Nora Atkinson's talk:
"Why Art Thrives at Burning Man"
2018

Also try Wanuri Kahiu's talk:
"Fun, Fierce and Fantastical African Art"
2017

LEARN TO PLAY AN INSTRUMENT

The very process of playing an instrument makes you more creative.

We'd all like to learn how to play a musical instrument, but many of us never get around to it. So here's some extra motivation: it will actually make you more creative in general.

That's not just a theory, but hard science. In her talk "How Playing an Instrument Benefits Your Brain," educator Anita Collins explains the conclusions neuroscientists have reached after hooking up human brains to instruments like functional magnetic resonance imaging (fMRI) and positron emission tomography (PET) scanners.

"Because making music also involves crafting and understanding its emotional content and message," Collins says, "musicians often have higher levels of executive function, a category of interlinked tasks that includes planning, strategizing, and attention to detail, and requires simultaneous analysis of both cognitive and emotional aspects."

Learning to play an instrument also helps to improve our memory. And most importantly, neuroscientists have *not* found similar results when analyzing people doing other activities—such as sports or painting. This suggests that playing an instrument really does offer a special path to being more creative.

Why might that be so? "The research is still fairly new, but neuroscientists have a pretty good idea," says Collins. "Playing a musical instrument engages practically every area of the brain at once, especially the visual, auditory, and motor cortices."

So, if you really want to give your brain a workout, creatively speaking, pick up that guitar, violin, or flute, and start making music!

Q FIND OUT MORE

Anita Collins's talk:
"How Playing an Instrument Benefits Your Brain"
2014

Also try Jeff Hao's talk:
"Learn Hao to Play the Piano in 10 Minutes"
2016

RETURN TO YOUR ROOTS

The community you came from can help unblock your creativity.

As the saying goes, "Write about what you know." But sometimes, that inspiration dries up. This is exactly what happened to Sting, as he explains in his talk "How I Started Writing Songs Again."

"One day, the songs stopped coming," he recalls. "And while you've suffered from periods of writer's block before, albeit briefly, this is something chronic . . . Days turned to weeks, and weeks to months, and pretty soon those months have turned into years with very little to show for your efforts."

How did Sting turn it around? Essentially, he realized that "what you know" doesn't strictly have to be about *you*. Instead, he decided to "sidestep his ego," go back to his roots, and seek inspiration from the people he'd grown up with.

That wasn't an easy process, and he recognizes the irony that "the landscape I'd worked so hard to escape from, and the community that I'd more or less abandoned and exiled myself from, should be the very landscape, the very community I would have to return to, to find my missing muse." But once he'd made that mental leap, he says, "the songs started to come thick and fast."

Like Sting, many creative people turn their back on the people and area they grew up in, and often for good reason. But the next time you suffer from creative block, ask yourself whether they could be the key to unlocking it. Discover more about how to draw on your heritage on page 164.

Q FIND OUT MORE

Sting's talk:
"How I Started Writing Songs Again"
2014

Also try Rich Venezia's talk:
"How to Grow Empathy from Uncovering Your Roots"
2017

PUSH YOUR BOUNDARIES

Go for broke and experiment wildly.

Most artists like to experiment from time to time. But are you really pushing yourself, and being as experimental as you can?

In her talk "Your Body Is My Canvas," visual artist Alexa Meade shows just how far it's possible to step outside the mainstream and develop an approach that's truly exciting and original. Rather than painting representations of people and objects, she skips the canvas altogether and applies the paint directly to *them*. "If I want to paint your portrait, I'm painting it on you, physically on you," she explains. "That also means you're probably going to end up with an earful of paint, because I need to paint your ear on your ear."

Everything in Meade's scenes, from people to furniture to food, gets covered in paint. "And in this way, I'm able to take a three-dimensional scene and make it look like a two-dimensional painting. I can photograph it from any angle, and it will still look 2-D."

Meade has been through a lot of trial and error to get this process right, of course. But she's had a lot of fun along the way, and it's opened her mind to a myriad of creative possibilities.

She concludes, "You can find the strange in the familiar, as long as you're willing to look beyond what's already been brought to light, that you can see what's below the surface, hiding in the shadows, and recognize that there can be more there than meets the eye."

Q FIND OUT MORE

Alexa Meade's talk:
"Your Body Is My Canvas"
2013

Also try Pawel Nolbert's talk:
"Evolution Through Experimentation"
2016

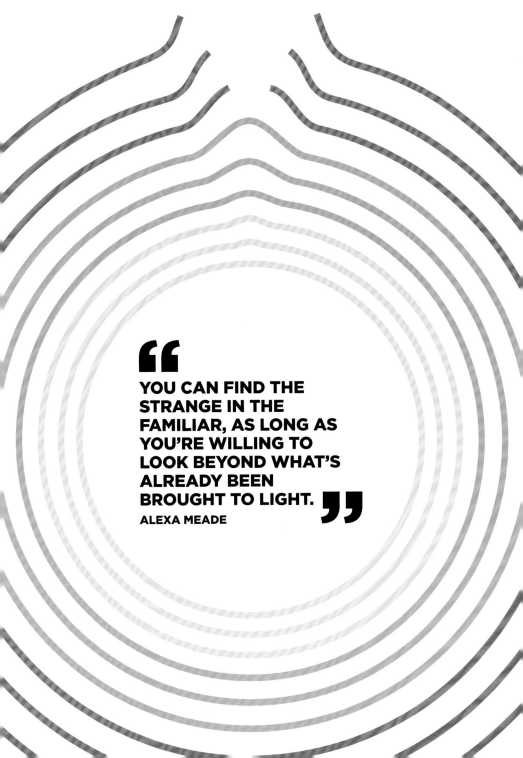

"YOU CAN FIND THE STRANGE IN THE FAMILIAR, AS LONG AS YOU'RE WILLING TO LOOK BEYOND WHAT'S ALREADY BEEN BROUGHT TO LIGHT."

ALEXA MEADE

DON'T CRITICIZE; PARODY

Poking fun can be a great outlet for your creative frustrations.

There's a long tradition of parody in the art world, from Andy Warhol to Banksy. But for a parody to work, there needs to be an underlying point to it. A great example is outlined in artist and curator Shea Hembrey's talk "How I Became 100 Artists."

Hembrey had spent months in Europe seeing the major international art exhibitions everyone was talking about, but they'd left him a little cold. "I was longing for more work that was appealing to a broad public, that was accessible," he explains. "And the second thing that I was longing for was some more exquisite craftsmanship and technique."

He could have just shared his frustrations in an article or social media post, but what would that have achieved? Instead, he decided to respond with an ambitious parody. He spent two years preparing an international art show that claimed to feature work from a hundred different artists—but in truth, he invented all of the artists and created all the artwork himself.

It was a bold and inventive strategy, and as you might expect, it got Hembrey a ton of attention in the international press. Next time you want to criticize something, think about whether you could parody it instead, and turn something negative into something positive and constructive.

FIND OUT MORE

Shea Hembrey's talk:
"How I Became 100 Artists"
2010

Also try Eireamhan Semple's talk:
"The Power of Satire"
2015

BE INVENTIVE
and generate great ideas

Searching for new ideas but coming up empty? This chapter explores a range of methods for coming up with inventive, game-changing notions.

PLAY A WORD GAME

Unlock your subconscious with simple word play.

Sometimes, ideas just won't come. Toy designer Shimpei Takahashi offers a potential solution in his talk "Play This Word Game to Come Up with Original Ideas."

The game involves saying words that start with the last letter of the previous word (such as apple, elephant, trumpet). It also works in Takahashi's native Japanese, and he gives the example of "*neko, kora, raibu, burashi*" (which translates as "cat, cola, live, brush").

But here's the twist: while you're playing the game, you need to think about the words on a secondary level. "You force those words to connect to what you want to think of, and form ideas," Takahashi explains. "In my case, for example, since I want to think of toys, what could a toy cat be? A cat that lands after doing a somersault from a high place? How about a toy with cola? A toy gun where you shoot cola and get someone soaking wet?"

The fact that these notions are ridiculous is kind of the point: the aim is to have fun and make unusual connections. "Keep them flowing," Takahashi stresses. "The more ideas you produce, [the more]

> **THE MORE IDEAS YOU PRODUCE, [THE MORE] YOU'RE SURE TO COME UP WITH SOME GOOD ONES, TOO.**
> **SHIMPEI TAKAHASHI**

you're sure to come up with some good ones, too.

"A brush, for example. Can we make a toothbrush into a toy? We could combine a toothbrush with a guitar, and you've got a toy you can play with while brushing your teeth. Kids who don't like to brush their teeth might begin to like it."

Q FIND OUT MORE

Shimpei Takahashi's talk: "Play This Word Game to Come Up with Original Ideas" 2013

Also try Ajit Narayanan's talk: "A Word Game to Communicate in Any Language" 2013

DITCH THE MENTAL SNOOZE BUTTON

To develop creative ideas, you must defy your natural reticence.

We're all looking for clever techniques to generate new creative ideas. In her talk "How to Stop Screwing Yourself Over," author, life coach, TV host, and CNN commentator Mel Robbins suggests that the answer may be far simpler. "Your problem isn't ideas," she says. "Your problem is you don't act on them. You kill them."

Robbins paints a picture that many of us—if we're honest—will recognize. "All day long you have ideas that could change your life, that could change the world, that could change the way that you feel," she says. "And what do you do with them? Nothing!"

What she calls "the inner snooze button" is the main culprit. "You have these amazing ideas that bubble up . . . like Ping-Pong balls—bam-bam-bam—and every time you have an idea, what do you do? Hit the snooze!"

Why don't we spring to action and start developing our ideas? Because we're waiting to be in the right mood. But that's an illusion, says Robbins. "There's one fact that you need to know," she stresses. "You are *never* going to feel like it. Ever. No one's coming, motivation isn't happening, you're never going to feel like it."

In short, the only way to make something happen is, in the words of Nike, to "Just do it." You need to make the leap, because no one else is going to make it for you.

> **YOUR PROBLEM ISN'T IDEAS. YOUR PROBLEM IS YOU DON'T ACT ON THEM.**
> MEL ROBBINS

Q FIND OUT MORE

Mel Robbins's talk:
"How to Stop Screwing Yourself Over"
2011

Also try Manav Subodh's talk:
"How to Activate Ideas"
2013

27/100
BE BORED

Kill your phone and see creativity come rushing back.

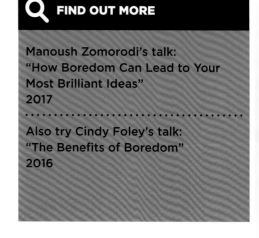

It's happened to most of us at some point in our lives. We'll be doing a menial task, like driving or folding laundry, when a really good idea hits us. As podcaster Manoush Zomorodi explains in her talk "How Boredom Can Lead to Your Most Brilliant Ideas," this happens because our brain starts forming new neural connections when our bodies are on autopilot.

Unfortunately, the constant distractions caused by digital technology mean we're spending less and less time in this "autopilot zone"—and getting fewer ideas as a result. Zomorodi wondered, "What would happen if we broke this vicious cycle?" So she asked her podcast listeners to actively spend less time on their phones and report what happened. "Immediately, we saw some creativity kick in," she recalls.

New Yorker Lisa Alpert was one of those taking part in the experiment. "I was bored, I guess," she recalls. "So, I suddenly looked at the stairway . . . and I thought, you know, I had just come down that stairway, but I could go back up and then come back down and get a little cardio . . . I did it ten times, and I had a complete cardio workout. I got on that R train feeling kind of exhausted, but, like, 'Wow, that had never occurred to me. How is that possible?'"

This is a small but significant proof of a simple concept: that if we put our phones away, our brains come up with more ideas. If you want to become more creative, says Zomorodi, "take a break, stare out the window, and know that by doing nothing you are actually being your most productive and creative self."

Q FIND OUT MORE

Manoush Zomorodi's talk: "How Boredom Can Lead to Your Most Brilliant Ideas" 2017

Also try Cindy Foley's talk: "The Benefits of Boredom" 2016

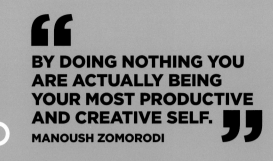

BY DOING NOTHING YOU ARE ACTUALLY BEING YOUR MOST PRODUCTIVE AND CREATIVE SELF.

MANOUSH ZOMORODI

DOODLE IN MEETINGS

Doodling is not a waste of time but a powerful tool.

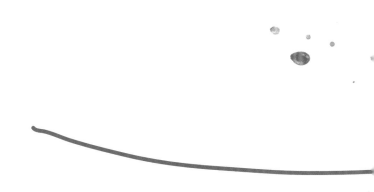

You're zoning out in a boring meeting, and suddenly you find yourself doodling on your notepad. Embarrassing, right? Wrong!

In fact, far from being a waste of time, doodling is actually a tried-and-tested way of processing information in a creative way. Many famous design works began as doodles, from the buildings of architect Frank Gehry to the Citibank logo designed by Pentagram's Paula Scher. And that's no accident.

As author and consultancy founder Sunni Brown explains in her talk "Doodlers Unite!," there are four ways to take in information in order to make decisions:

reading and writing, visual, auditory, and tactile. And the incredible thing about doodling, explains Brown, is that "it engages all four learning modalities simultaneously, with the possibility of an emotional experience. That is a pretty solid contribution for a behavior equated with doing nothing."

Our course, Brown recognizes this is not the popular view. "Our culture is so intensely focused on verbal information that we're almost blinded to the value of doodling," she admits. "[But] here's the truth: doodling is an incredibly powerful tool . . . It can be leveraged as a portal through which we move people into higher levels of visual literacy. My friends, the

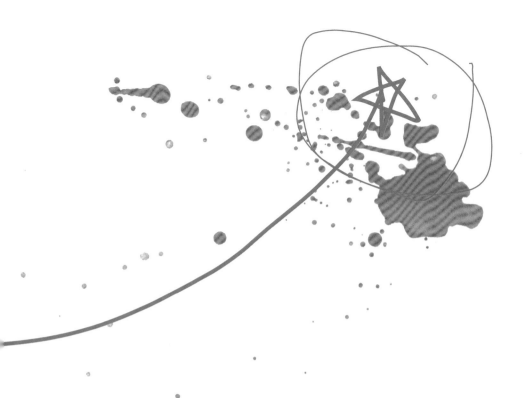

doodle has never been the nemesis of intellectual thought. In reality, it is one of its greatest allies." In other words, doodle to your heart's content. It could be the key to a creative breakthrough.

> ## IT ENGAGES ALL FOUR LEARNING MODALITIES SIMULTANEOUSLY, WITH THE POSSIBILITY OF AN EMOTIONAL EXPERIENCE.

SUNNI BROWN

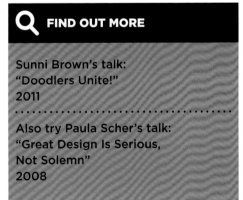

Q FIND OUT MORE

Sunni Brown's talk:
"Doodlers Unite!"
2011

Also try Paula Scher's talk:
"Great Design Is Serious,
Not Solemn"
2008

ASK A KID

From the mouths of babes . . .

 We all know from personal experience that children's imaginations are boundless and unlimited. So, why not take advantage of this, and ask kids to help with your creative process? In her talk "What Adults Can Learn from Kids," Adora Svitak, a short-story writer and blogger, gives an example.

"The Museum of Glass in Tacoma, Washington, has a program called Kids Design Glass, and kids draw their own ideas for glass art," she explains. "The resident artists said they got some of their best ideas from the program, because kids don't think about the limitations of how hard it can be to blow glass into certain shapes, they just think of good ideas. Now, when you think of glass, you might think of colorful Chihuly designs, or maybe Italian vases, but kids challenge glass artists to go beyond that, into the realm of brokenhearted snakes and bacon boys."

Why doesn't this kind of ideas exchange happen more often? The answer is that adults underestimate kids' abilities. "We love challenges, but when expectations are low, trust me, we will sink to them," Svitak says. So don't fall into the same trap: find ways to draw on children's ideas, and you'll soon be learning from each other.

> **THE RESIDENT ARTISTS . . . GOT SOME OF THEIR BEST IDEAS FROM THE PROGRAM, BECAUSE KIDS DON'T THINK ABOUT THE LIMITATIONS.**
> **ADORA SVITAK**

Q FIND OUT MORE

Adora Svitak's talk:
"What Adults Can Learn from Kids"
2010

Also try Thomas Suarez's talk:
"A 12-year-old App Developer"
2011

TURN OUT THE LIGHTS

In darkness, our imaginations light up.

If you want to think in a different way, head for the light switch. Because as archaeologist Holley Moyes describes in her talk "How Darkness Influences Imagination," humans have always sought darkness to transcend the ordinary.

Knowing that caves have been important to religious rites throughout history, Moyes carried out an experiment to find out the psychological role that darkness plays in such events. This involved presenting students with a number of impossible-sounding scenarios and asking them to come up with possible explanations.

Half of the students were placed in a well-lit room with a picture window, and the other half were taken to a dark room with only a tiny light. Moyes found that "in the light room people tended to choose more rational or scientific explanations, but in the dark room people were more inclined to use their imaginary thinking."

This study echoes anthropological research carried out by Polly Wiessner, who recorded conversations with the Kalahari Bushmen over a twenty-year period. "During the day, people wanted to talk about ordinary things: where are they gonna go, what are they gonna do, what are they gonna eat, things like this. But at

> **" IN THE DARK ROOM PEOPLE WERE MORE INCLINED TO USE THEIR IMAGINARY THINKING. "**
> **HOLLEY MOYES**

night it was totally different: sitting around the fire, they sang, they danced, and eighty percent of the time they told stories . . . living in their imaginary thinking."

Moyes's conclusion? "When we take the archaeological record . . . what it suggests is that our environment plays a very important part, in not only how we feel, how we think, but also how we interpret our world." The next time you want to bring your imagination to life, a simple remedy therefore presents itself: turn down or, better still, turn off the lights.

🔍 FIND OUT MORE

Holley Moyes's talk:
"How Darkness Influences Imagination"
2016

. . . .

Also try Diane Knutson's talk:
"Why We Need Darkness"
2016

FIND NEW CREATIVE IDEAS IN THE MARGINS

Learn to use your peripheral vision.

Great design is often associated with grand gestures, but it doesn't need to be. As British branding and design guru Paul Bennett explains in his talk "Design Is in the Details," it's often about solving small, overlooked universal problems.

Bennett quotes the Buddha as saying: "Finding yourself in the margins, looking to the edges of things, is often a really interesting place to start." And when it comes to design work, he offers some concrete examples of what that looks like in practice.

Driving home one night, British inventor Percy Shaw saw the reflection of his car headlights in the eyes of a cat at the side of the road, and that led to him creating the cat's eye road stud. One Saturday morning, American TV producer Joan Ganz Cooney saw her daughter watching the test card, waiting for her

shows to start, and from that came *Sesame Street*. Swiss electrical engineer George de Mestral was walking his dog in a field and got covered in prickly burrs, and that gave him the idea for Velcro.

All these stories are about people who looked at the world in a new and different way. As Bennett puts it, it's all about "using your eyes, seeing things for the first time, seeing things afresh and using them as an opportunity to create new possibilities."

So remove your metaphorical blinkers, take a fresh look at the world, and see what new ideas come to mind.

Q FIND OUT MORE

Paul Bennett's talk:
"Design Is in the Details"
2005

Also try Luc de Brabandere's talk:
"Reinventing Creative Thinking"
2015

**LOOKING TO THE EDGES
OF THINGS IS OFTEN A
REALLY INTERESTING
PLACE TO START.**
PAUL BENNETT

UNCOVER IDEAS THROUGH IMPROVISATION

Struggling to begin? Write the first sentence, then improvise.

 Creative ideas don't always come fully formed. Sometimes you start with just a fragment and see where it takes you.

In his talk "Be an Artist, Right Now!," Young-ha Kim recalls how twentieth-century novelist Franz Kafka began *The Metamorphosis* with these words: "One morning, as Gregor Samsa was waking up from anxious dreams, he discovered that in his bed he had been changed into a monstrous verminous bug."

By conjuring up such a bizarre sentence, and then continuing to write in order to justify it, Kafka crafted a novel that became a true classic. And Kim says this approach can work for any kind of creativity.

"[It's] about going a little nuts and justifying the next sentence," he explains. "Which is not much different from what a kid does. A kid who has just started to lie is taking the first step as a storyteller." And it's not just novelists who tell stories: artists do too.

Kim gives two examples: Pablo Picasso sticking handlebars into a bike seat and calling it *Bull's Head*, and Marcel Duchamp placing a urinal on its side and calling it *Fountain*. "Filling the gap between explanation and a weird act with stories: that's indeed what contemporary art is all about," Kim explains.

Even if we're not trained, we can all be artists, Kim stresses. We just need to reboot our inner child, start telling stories—the more ridiculous the better—and proceed to create new and exciting work.

Q FIND OUT MORE

Young-ha Kim's talk: "Be an Artist, Right Now!" 2010

Also try Mihaly Csikszentmihalyi's talk: "Flow, the Secret to Happiness" 2004

LOCATE NEW IDEAS IN YOUR SUBCONSCIOUS

Don't overthink things: let your instincts take over.

 When it comes to generating fresh ideas, sometimes it pays not to overthink. Indeed, according to Jay Silver, a maker research scientist at Intel Labs, sometimes it's best not to think at all.

In his talk "Hack a Banana, Make a Keyboard!," Silver recalls his experience at a camp for teenagers. He suggested they go into the woods near a stream and "just put stuff together, you know, make something." And soon, they were fashioning intricate and interesting works of art.

One of them was asked how he got his sticks to stay on a tree. His reply was, "I don't know, but I can show you." And this, for Silver, was a truly eye-opening moment.

"His hands know and his intuition knows," Silver points out. And this led the youngster to create something outside of his normal inner restrictions, because "sometimes what we know gets in the way of what could be."

Later, Silver tried a similar approach with his own son, giving him non-rectilinear cactus building blocks, but not showing him how to use them. "And so he's like, 'Okay, I'll just mess around with this.' . . . And before long, he's got this mechanism where you can almost launch and catapult objects around."

The lesson? If we don't plan or understand too much about what we're doing, we might make something incredible as a result.

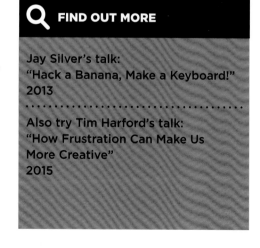

🔍 FIND OUT MORE

Jay Silver's talk:
"Hack a Banana, Make a Keyboard!"
2013

Also try Tim Harford's talk:
"How Frustration Can Make Us More Creative"
2015

WHY CHEAPER IDEAS OFTEN WORK BEST

Don't waste your money on expensive approaches.

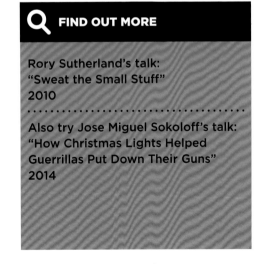

Big problems seem to demand big solutions. But advertising executive Rory Sutherland believes that flashy, expensive fixes are often a distraction. You can usually do more with less.

In his talk "Sweat the Small Stuff," he offers an amusing example from Virgin Atlantic's upper-class section. The salt and pepper containers it offers its passengers are beautifully designed, and tempting to steal. But when you pick them up and look underneath, you see the engraved words "Pinched from Virgin Atlantic." That's something you'll never forget, Sutherland argues. "Years after you remember the strategic question of whether you're flying in a 777 or an Airbus, you remember those words and that experience."

Sutherland also cites the lift in the Lydmar Hotel, Stockholm, which allows you to choose your own lift music. "My guess is that the cost of installing this is probably £500–1,000 [$600–1,200] max," he says. "It's frankly more memorable than all those millions of hotels we've all stayed at, that tell you that your room has actually been recently renovated at a cost of $500,000."

He admits that it's human nature to want to be associated with big-money projects. "And yet, what behavioral economics shows time after time after time is . . . that actually what changes our behavior, and what changes our attitude to things, is not actually proportionate to the degree of expense."

So, ditch the pricier ideas, and focus on cheap and clever ones instead. They'll probably be much more effective.

Q FIND OUT MORE

Rory Sutherland's talk: "Sweat the Small Stuff" 2010

Also try Jose Miguel Sokoloff's talk: "How Christmas Lights Helped Guerrillas Put Down Their Guns" 2014

WHAT CHANGES OUR BEHAVIOR IS NOT ACTUALLY PROPORTIONATE TO THE DEGREE OF EXPENSE.

RORY SUTHERLAND

BE FOCUSED
in refining your ideas

Generating new ideas is one thing; putting them into practice and creating something that people will love is another. This chapter looks at bringing a great idea to fruition.

DISCOVER WHAT CUSTOMERS REALLY WANT

Reach the right solution by "paving over desire paths."

> **DESIRE PATHS ARE GOING TO SPRING UP FASTER THAN EVER. OUR JOB IS TO PICK THE APPROPRIATE ONES AND PAVE OVER THEM.**
>
> **TOM HULME**

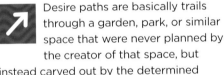 Desire paths are basically trails through a garden, park, or similar space that were never planned by the creator of that space, but instead carved out by the determined footsteps of people walking through it. And their existence points to an uncomfortable truth: that what we create isn't always what the public actually wants.

In his talk "What Can We Learn from Shortcuts?," British designer Tom Hulme offers the example of the obligatory walk through Heathrow Airport's duty-free section. "It was amazing to me how many people refused to take the long, meandering path to the left, and just cut through to the right," he says.

But creatives needn't be frustrated by desire paths; instead, they can use them to their benefit. Hulme gives the example of the University of California, Berkeley, where the architects simply built the buildings, waited a few months for desire paths to form naturally, and then paved over them.

Similarly, Boston entrepreneur Ayr Muir knew he wanted to open a restaurant, but didn't know where. "[So] he launched a service, in this case a food truck, and he changed the location each day. He'd write a different menu on the side in a whiteboard marker to figure out what people wanted. He now has a chain of restaurants."

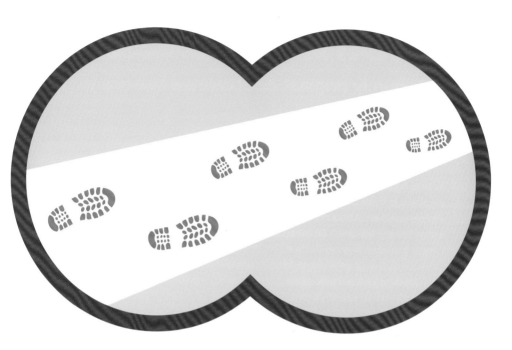

A more metaphorical take on desire paths can be found in website and app design, where there's usually a mountain of data about how users behave, and this can be used to improve the service.

Whatever you use them for, Hulme believes that desire paths will play a central role in the future of creativity. "The world is incredibly flux at the moment. It's changing constantly," he says. "These desire paths are going to spring up faster than ever. Our job is to pick the appropriate ones and pave over them."

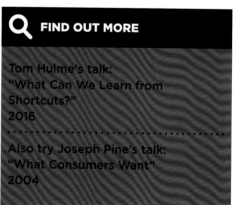

Q FIND OUT MORE

Tom Hulme's talk:
"What Can We Learn from Shortcuts?"
2016

. . . .

Also try Joseph Pine's talk:
"What Consumers Want"
2004

WALK THE LINE BETWEEN INSPIRATION AND COPYING

No idea is purely original, but there's a balance to be struck.

Artists have always taken inspiration from others. The Sex Pistols used an Abba riff in their song "Pretty Vacant," Shakespeare based his most famous play on Arthur Brooke's poem *The Tragicall Historye of Romeus and Juliet*, and Banksy's early work was strongly reminiscent of the stenciled graffiti of Blek Le Rat. The list goes on . . .

But there's a line between "remixing," where an artist brings something new to the table, and "recycling," where they just blatantly copy someone. And it's a line often crossed by those in the music industry, says producer Mark Ronson in his talk "How Sampling Transformed Music."

When sampling is done well by the likes of Fat Boy Slim—who takes slivers of obscure recordings and splices them into a larger tune—it can be wonderfully creative. "[But] all of a sudden everyone's taking these massive eighties tunes like Bowie's 'Let's Dance' . . . and just rapping on them," Ronson complains.

"You can't just hijack nostalgia wholesale," he argues. "It leaves the listener feeling sickly . . . You have to take an element of those things and then bring something fresh and new to it." He points to Miley Cyrus's sample of Doug E. Fresh and Slick Rick's "La Di Da Di" on her song "We Can't Stop" as an example of how to do it right.

What applies to music applies to every other creative discipline. Don't be scared of taking inspiration from others, but do try to create something original as a result.

🔍 FIND OUT MORE

Mark Ronson's talk: "How Sampling Transformed Music" 2014

Also try Meklit Hadero's talk: "The Unexpected Beauty of Everyday Sounds" 2015

GET INSPIRED IN UNEXPECTED PLACES

It's not just your own profession that can inspire you.

It's good to take inspiration from other creatives. But the influence doesn't have to be direct, such as one painter being inspired by another. It can be a lot more subtle than that.

In his talk "Can Design Save Newspapers?," Polish designer Jacek Utko recalls how sales of traditional print newspapers began to fall rapidly in the internet era. It was a thorny problem, but then he found inspiration in one of the most unexpected places.

Utko was out one night in London, enjoying a performance by the maverick circus troupe Cirque du Soleil, when he had a revelation. "I thought, 'These guys took some creepy, run-down entertainment, and [raised] it to the highest possible level of performance art . . . Oh my God, maybe I can do the same with these boring newspapers!'"

And he did. "We started to redesign them, one by one. The front page became our signature. It was my personal intimate channel to talk to the readers." As a result of this new design-led approach, sales stopped declining and actually started going up.

It seems slightly crazy that what turned things around wasn't Utko analyzing his competitors, or even other forms of media, but a bunch of chainsaw- and flamethrower-wielding French circus performers. If we all looked for inspiration in such nonobvious places, could we find game-changing solutions too?

FIND OUT MORE

Jacek Utko's talk:
"Can Design Save Newspapers?"
2009

Also try Naif Al-Mutawa's talk:
"Superheroes Inspired by Islam"
2010

USE EMOTION TO MAKE YOUR DESIGNS BETTER

Being true to yourself is the key to great work.

The more our world goes digital, the more focus creatives are putting on technology. But in his talk "Design and Discovery," graphic designer David Carson reminds us that tech is still only a tool. To create anything truly worthwhile, we ultimately need to look inside ourselves.

Why? Because for a design to communicate a message, it needs to be more than just logical and legible: it needs to engage the viewer on an emotional level.

Carson gives a range of examples, including a cover he designed for the rock band Nine Inch Nails shortly after 9/11, featuring the view from the bottom of a bomb shelter. He also discusses a fly poster campaign for the Coalition for a Smoke-free Environment that made a big impact thanks to its snarky payoff line: "If the cigarette companies can lie, then so can we."

You can only give emotional weight to your work if you're true to yourself, Carson stresses. "You have to utilize who you are. Nobody else can pull from your background, from your parents, your upbringing, your whole life experience. If you allow that to happen, it's really the only way you can do some unique work, and you're going to enjoy the work a lot more as well."

Q FIND OUT MORE

David Carson's talk:
"Design and Discovery"
2003

Also try Eric Berridge's talk:
"Why Tech Needs the Humanities"
2017

YOU HAVE TO UTILIZE WHO YOU ARE. NOBODY ELSE CAN PULL FROM YOUR BACKGROUND, FROM YOUR PARENTS, YOUR UPBRINGING.

DAVID CARSON

IMPROVE YOUR WORK BY SIMPLIFYING IT

Abstraction is a quick and easy way to make any creative work better.

Struggling to make your creative idea work in the way you want it to? One tried-and-tested way to do this is to try to simplify it.

In his talk "You Are Fluent in This Language (And Don't Even Know It)," illustrator Christoph Niemann explains how he does this in art, through a process called "abstraction."

"I try to achieve a level of simplicity where, if you were to take away one more element, the whole concept would just collapse," he explains. And he's even come up with a system for doing so, which he calls call the abstract-o-meter.

"You take a symbol, any symbol—for example, the heart and the arrow," he explains. "Now, if I go too realistic on it, it just grosses everybody out. If I go too far on the other side and do very abstract, nobody has any idea what they're looking at. So I have to find the perfect place on that scale. In this case, it's somewhere in the middle."

Once you've reduced an image to its simplest form, all sorts of new connections and possibilities become possible. And it's an approach that can work in other media too.

Does your novel feel slow and boring? Try cutting out a quarter of the words. Multi-instrumental song not working? Try playing it on an acoustic guitar and see how it sounds then. You might be surprised how often simplifying a piece of creative work will make it better.

Q FIND OUT MORE

Christoph Niemann's talk: "You Are Fluent in This Language (And Don't Even Know It)" 2018

Also try John Maeda's talk: "Designing for Simplicity" 2007

"
I TRY TO ACHIEVE A LEVEL OF SIMPLICITY WHERE, IF YOU WERE TO TAKE AWAY ONE MORE ELEMENT, THE WHOLE CONCEPT WOULD JUST COLLAPSE. "

CHRISTOPH NIEMANN

GET CREATIVE WITH SMART MATERIALS

Harness the latest tech to develop something incredible.

> **WE OFTEN TACKLE PROBLEMS FROM UNCONVENTIONAL ANGLES, AND, IN THE PROCESS, END UP DISCOVERING ALTERNATIVES OR EVEN BETTER WAYS TO DO THINGS.**
> **CATARINA MOTA**

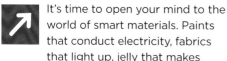

It's time to open your mind to the world of smart materials. Paints that conduct electricity, fabrics that light up, jelly that makes music, glass that turns from clear to opaque—all these things exist now, says maker Catarina Mota in her talk "Play with Smart Materials," and they're ready and waiting for us to play with them.

It's not just about having fun, but creating genuinely brilliant things. For example, thermochromic pigments that change color at a given temperature can be used on baby bottles to indicate when the contents are cool enough to drink.

And be aware that you're not alone. To help you start experimenting, Mota and fellow maker Kirsty Boyle have begun a project called OpenMaterials, which you can access at openmaterials.org. "It's a website where we, and anyone else who wants to join us, share experiments, publish information, encourage others to contribute whenever they can, and aggregate resources," Mota explains.

Importantly, you don't have to be an expert. "Innovation has always been fueled by tinkerers," she points out. "Amateurs, not experts, have been the inventors and improvers of things ranging from mountain

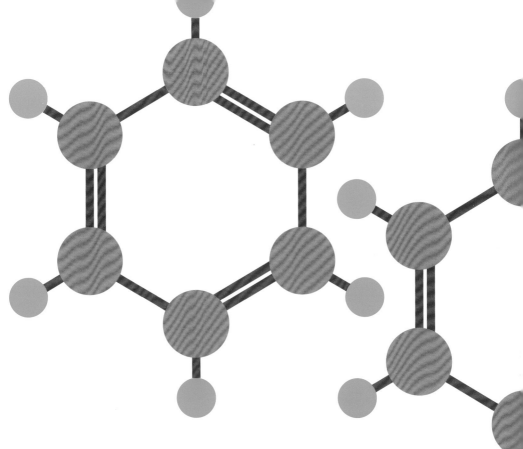

bikes to semiconductors, personal computers, airplanes." Nor do you necessarily need expensive equipment; primarily, you just need determination.

"The interesting thing about makers is that we create out of passion and curiosity, and we're not afraid to fail," Mota stresses. "We often tackle problems from unconventional angles, and, in the process, end up discovering alternatives or even better ways to do things."

Why not take the plunge and join the maker revolution? And learn more about how to use new tech to boost your creativity on page 122.

FIND OUT MORE

Catarina Mota's talk:
"Play with Smart Materials"
2012
. . . .
Also try Doris Kim Sung's talk:
"Metal that Breathes"
2012

GET ORIGINAL IDEAS FROM DISABILITY

By making your designs accessible to all, everyone benefits.

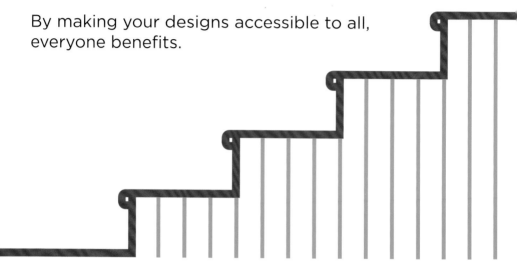

Taking into account people with disabilities when you design something is obviously the ethical thing to do. But it's more than that. As the title of Elise Roy's talk makes clear, "When We Design for Disability, We All Benefit."

The artist and designer explains how being deaf gives her a unique way of experiencing and reframing the world. "My observation skills have been honed so that I pick up on things that others would never pick up on," she says. "My constant need to adapt has made me a great 'ideator' and problem solver. And I've often had to do this within limitations and constraints. This is something that designers also have to deal with frequently."

Whether or not you have a disability yourself, just understanding the challenges people with disabilities face can spark the most original and inventive ideas. Take the OXO potato peeler. "It was originally designed for people with arthritis, but it was so comfortable, everybody loved it," Roy points out. "Text messaging—that was originally designed for people who are deaf, and as you know, everybody loves that, too."

Her conclusion? "When we design for disability first, we often stumble upon solutions that are . . . often better than when we design for the norm." And what designer wouldn't want that?

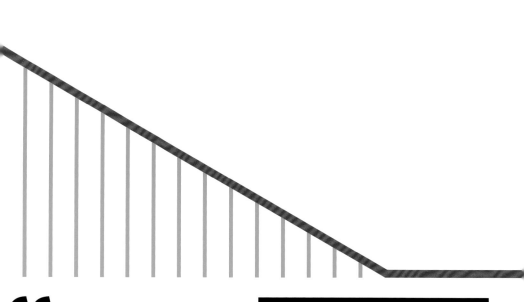

> **WHEN WE DESIGN FOR DISABILITY FIRST, WE OFTEN STUMBLE UPON SOLUTIONS THAT ARE ... OFTEN BETTER THAN WHEN WE DESIGN FOR THE NORM.**
> **ELISE ROY**

🔍 FIND OUT MORE

Elise Roy's talk:
"When We Design for Disability,
We All Benefit"
2008

· ·

Also try Emilie Weight's talk:
"Three Things I Learned from My
Intellectually Disabled Son"
2017

HARNESS DARK FEELINGS TO BE MORE CREATIVE

Bad experiences can inspire your best work.

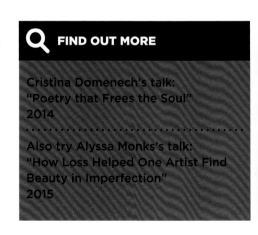

As we discussed on page 74, drawing emotions can benefit our creative work hugely. And that can apply especially to our darkest feelings. Mary Shelley wrote *Frankenstein* against the backdrop of a massive volcanic eruption that led to crop failures and starvation across Europe. Walt Disney created Mickey Mouse in a fit of rage, after legal action had sent him careering toward bankruptcy. The accidental death of Eric Clapton's four-year-old son inspired "Tears in Heaven," one of his most beautiful and beloved songs.

Drawing on difficult emotions in our creative work can also be a very therapeutic way to deal with those feelings and turn them into something positive. And you don't even have to be a professional to do so.

In her talk "Poetry that Frees the Soul," Cristina Domenech explains how she teaches writing at an Argentinian prison, to help inmates express and understand themselves better.

"It's said that to be a poet you have to go to hell and back. And they have plenty of hell. Plenty of hell," she explains.

"So we started appropriating that hell; we plunged ourselves, headfirst, into the seventh circle. And in that seventh circle of hell, our very own, beloved circle, they learned that they could make the walls invisible, that they could make the windows yell, and that we could hide inside the shadows."

You may not have anything like the personal demons of these inmates, but we all have our dark emotions and bad memories. Dig deep, draw on them, and you might just make something transformational as a result.

🔍 FIND OUT MORE

Cristina Domenech's talk:
"Poetry that Frees the Soul"
2014

Also try Alyssa Monks's talk:
"How Loss Helped One Artist Find Beauty in Imperfection"
2015

IT'S SAID THAT TO BE A POET YOU HAVE TO GO TO HELL AND BACK.

CRISTINA DOMENECH

ATTRACT ATTENTION BY REMOVING ELEMENTS

Taking things away from your art will pique people's interest.

Want to engage people with your art on a deeper level? Hiding expected elements can be a surprisingly effective way to do it. Chinese artist Liu Bolin specializes in using chameleon-like methods to make himself, and other people, disappear into his environments. You can find them in his pictures, but only if you look closely.

As he explains in his talk "The Invisible Man," he doesn't just do this to amuse, but to draw attention to hidden injustices. He gives the example of his piece *Xia Gang* (*Leaving Post*, a Chinese euphemism for "laid off"). It refers to the 21.3 million people who lost their jobs between 1998 and 2000 during China's transition from a planned economy to a market economy.

"The six people in the photo are *xia gang* workers," Liu explains. "I made them invisible in the deserted shop where they had lived and worked all their lives . . . We can only see six men in this picture, but in fact, those who are hidden here are all people who were laid off. They have just been made invisible." By making the audience work to find them in the picture, Liu drives that point home powerfully.

The important thing, he stresses, is to have a point of view that you have thought through clearly and carefully. "When I work on a new piece, I pay more attention to the expression of ideas. For instance, why would I make myself invisible? What will making myself invisible here cause people to think?"

"IF AN ARTWORK IS TO TOUCH SOMEONE, IT MUST BE THE RESULT OF NOT ONLY TECHNIQUE, BUT ALSO THE ARTIST'S THINKING."
LIU BOLIN

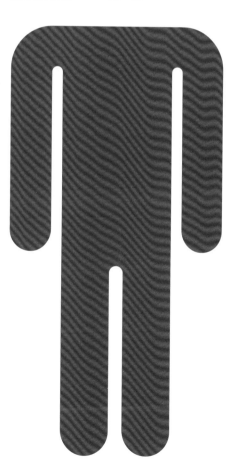

He continues, "I think that in art, an artist's attitude is the most important element. If an artwork is to touch someone, it must be the result of not only technique, but also the artist's thinking and struggle in life."

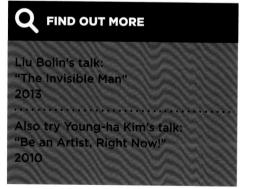

🔍 **FIND OUT MORE**

Liu Bolin's talk:
"The Invisible Man"
2013

· ·

Also try Young-ha Kim's talk:
"Be an Artist, Right Now!"
2010

RAISE CREATIVITY BY HARNESSING STILLNESS

Travel broadens the mind, but so does going nowhere.

We often think that we need a vacation in order to recharge our creative batteries. But that doesn't always work. As travel writer Pico Iyer explains, "One of the first things you learn when you travel is that nowhere is magical unless you can bring the right eyes to it. You take an angry man to the Himalayas, he just starts complaining about the food."

In his talk "The Art of Stillness," Iyer offers an alternative suggestion: going nowhere. That might sound strange, but he points out that in a world of constant movement and distraction, staying put and practicing stillness can be far more relaxing than going on a trip.

By "stillness," he's not talking about anything radical or outlandish. "I mean nothing more intimidating than taking a few minutes out of every day, or a few days out of every season," he explains.

"This is what wise beings through the centuries from every tradition have been telling us . . . More than 2,000 years ago, the Stoics were reminding us it's not our experience that makes our lives, it's what we do with it."

So why not give it a try? After all, as Iyer explains, "In an age of acceleration, nothing can be more exhilarating than going slow. And in an age of distraction, nothing is so luxurious as paying attention. And in an age of constant movement, nothing is so urgent as sitting still."

Q FIND OUT MORE

Pico Iyer's talk:
"The Art of Stillness"
2014
. . . .
Also try Andy Puddicombe's talk:
"All It Takes Is 10 Mindful Minutes"
2012

TELL BETTER STORIES USING LETTER DESIGN

The shape and style of letters conveys much more than their literal meaning.

Searching for ways to bring your design to life? Then don't underestimate the power of lettering.

In her talk "The Secret Language of Letter Design," Argentinian graphic designer Martina Flor discusses how the shape and design of letters visually speaks to the viewer in ways that transcend the actual words they spell.

"They send us to different eras, they convey values, they tell us stories," she explains. "Some letters tell us that something is modern, or at least that it was back in the seventies. Others verify the importance and monumentality of a place . . . [or] make us imagine what a place looks like inside."

Flor recalls how she got playful with lettering when designing an *Alice in Wonderland* cover. "What if, to communicate the idea of wonder, I used my best handwriting, with lots of curlicues here and there? Or what if I focused more on the fact that the book is a classic, and used more conventional lettering? . . . Or how would it look, considering this book has so much

gibberish, if I combined both universes in a single arrangement: rigid letters and smooth letters living together?"

There are no "right answers" to such questions or "correct ways" of doing things, but that's kind of the point. Lettering offers an endless variety of possibilities if we open our minds to them. Above all, remember Flor's words: "If the message is important, it requires work and craftsmanship. And if the reader is important, they deserve beauty and fantasy as well."

Q FIND OUT MORE

Martina Flor's talk: "The Secret Language of Letter Design" 2016

Also try Chip Kidd's talk: "Designing Books Is No Laughing Matter. OK, It Is" 2012

GET A NEW PERSPECTIVE BY TAKING TEN MINUTES

A few mindful minutes is all you need to reboot your brain.

When a computer starts slowing down and crashing, we know what to do: switch it off, and switch it on again. Nine times out of ten, it starts working perfectly again.

As mindfulness expert Andy Puddicombe explains in his talk "All It Takes Is 10 Mindful Minutes," you can do a similar thing with your brain. It's all about refreshing yourself for ten minutes a day, simply by meditating and experiencing the present moment.

Many people think meditation is about emptying your mind of thoughts and getting rid of emotions, but that's not quite right, says Puddicombe. "It's more about stepping back; sort of seeing the thought clearly, witnessing it coming and going, emotions coming and going without judgment, but with a relaxed, focused mind."

In this way, we can start to let go of the things that are most troubling us. "Meditation offers the opportunity, the potential to step back and to get a different perspective, to see that things aren't always as they appear," explains Puddicombe. "We can't change every little

thing that happens to us in life, but we can change the way that we experience it . . . so that you get to experience a greater sense of focus, calm, and clarity."

"

YOU GET TO EXPERIENCE A GREATER SENSE OF FOCUS, CALM, AND CLARITY. **"**

ANDY PUDDICOMBE

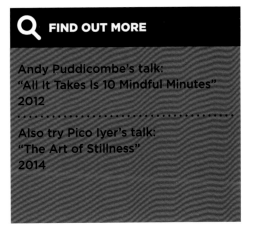

🔍 FIND OUT MORE

Andy Puddicombe's talk:
"All It Takes Is 10 Mindful Minutes"
2012

Also try Pico Iyer's talk:
"The Art of Stillness"
2014

USE CREATIVE SYSTEMS FROM DISTANT ERAS

Systems from the deep past can be hidden gems.

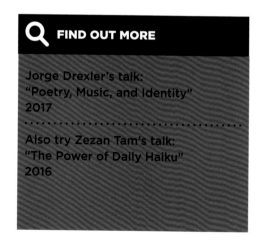

If you're struggling to find a way forward in developing your creative idea, try drawing on the deep past for inspiration. In his talk "Poetry, Music, and Identity," Oscar-winning Uruguayan musician Jorge Drexler recalls how he tried to write a song using an ancient system known as the décima. And it led him down a surprisingly fresh creative path.

Invented in 1591 by Spanish musician Vicente Espinel, this complex song form consists of forty-four lines: an introductory four-line stanza, followed by four ten-line stanzas. And despite spreading across the globe over the centuries, the system has remained surprisingly robust.

"It maintains even today, 400 years after its creation, exactly the same rhyme, syllable, and line structure," Drexler explains. "I applaud Vicente Espinel, because here it is, 426 years later, and the décima lives on everywhere in its original state."

And for good reason, it seems. Because taking on the décima challenge inspired Drexler to write "The Milonga of the Jewish Moor," a passionate call for peace in the Holy Land, and one of his most powerful and moving songs to date.

Could working within a similar traditional system—whether that be the décima, the haiku, the tanka, or something similar—provide the shot in the arm you need to develop your own creative ideas?

Q FIND OUT MORE

Jorge Drexler's talk:
"Poetry, Music, and Identity"
2017

Also try Zezan Tam's talk:
"The Power of Daily Haiku"
2016

> **[THE DÉCIMA] MAINTAINS EVEN TODAY, 400 YEARS AFTER ITS CREATION, EXACTLY THE SAME RHYME, SYLLABLE, AND LINE STRUCTURE.**
>
> **JORGE DREXLER**

BE COLLABORATIVE and get the right people involved

The best creative ideas often stem from the synergy of collaboration. This chapter examines how to choose the right people to team up with, and how to get the best out of them.

LEARN TO COLLABORATE WITH INTROVERTS

Some of the most creative people are introverts. Here's how to work with them.

Introverts don't get great press, because most organizations are designed in ways that make it difficult for them to succeed. But if you're looking for someone to collaborate with, an introvert could be the perfect choice.

In her talk "The Power of Introverts," author and introvert Susan Cain begins by pointing out that introversion is not the same as shyness. "Shyness is about fear of social judgment," she explains. "Introversion is more about how do you respond to stimulation, including social stimulation. So, extroverts really crave large amounts of stimulation, whereas introverts feel at their most alive, and their most switched on and their most capable, when they're in quieter, more low-key environments."

Because solitude is such an important ingredient in creativity, some of history's most creative people have been introverted. "Darwin, he took long walks alone in the woods and emphatically turned down dinner party invitations," Cain explains. "Theodor Geisel, better known as Dr. Seuss, he dreamed up many of his amazing creations in a lonely bell tower office . . . Steve Wozniak invented the first Apple computer sitting alone in his cubicle in Hewlett-Packard."

> # DR. SEUSS ... DREAMED UP MANY OF HIS AMAZING CREATIONS IN A LONELY BELL TOWER OFFICE.
> **SUSAN CAIN**

That doesn't mean introverts, of course, can't work with other people. Wozniak's collaboration with Steve Jobs is an obvious example of how an extrovert and introvert can work together. The important thing is that you build solitude and space into your working relationship with an introvert, to get the best out of them.

As Cain puts it, "Much better for everybody to go off by themselves, generate their own ideas freed from the distortions of group dynamics, and then come together as a team, to talk them through in a well-managed environment and take it from there."

🔍 FIND OUT MORE

Susan Cain's talk:
"The Power of Introverts"
2012
....
Also try Katherine Lucas's talk:
"In Defense of Extroverts"
2015

THE SECRET TO HIRING THE BEST PEOPLE

It's not just about the résumé.

When we're hiring for a creative team, it's tempting to pick someone purely on the basis of a great résumé. But human resources expert Regina Hartley takes quite a different approach.

"My colleagues and I created very official terms to describe two distinct categories of candidates," she explains. "We call A, the Silver Spoon: the one who clearly had advantages and was destined for success. And we call B, the Scrapper, the one who had to fight against tremendous odds to get to the same point."

Hartley doesn't hold anything against the Silver Spoon, noting that "getting into and graduating from an elite university takes a lot of hard work and sacrifice." But if your whole life has been engineered toward success, she wonders, how will you handle the tough times?

"One person I hired felt that, because he attended an elite university, there were certain assignments that were beneath him, like temporarily doing manual labor to better understand an operation," she recalls. "Eventually, he quit."

For this reason, Hartley always wants at least to give an interview to the Scrapper, who she describes as someone whose "whole life is destined for failure" and yet they still actually succeed.

"Take this résumé," she says. "This guy's parents give him up for adoption. He never finishes college. He job-hops quite a bit, goes on a sojourn to India for a year, and to top it off, he has dyslexia. Would you hire this guy? His name is Steve Jobs."

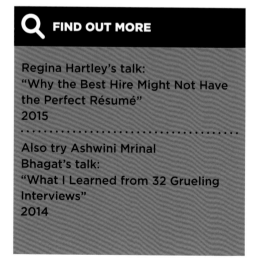

🔍 FIND OUT MORE

Regina Hartley's talk:
"Why the Best Hire Might Not Have the Perfect Résumé"
2015
. . . .
Also try Ashwini Mrinal Bhagat's talk:
"What I Learned from 32 Grueling Interviews"
2014

HOW TO EXPAND YOUR NETWORK

It's all about avoiding easy choices.

 Why should we expand our social circle? In her talk "The Secret to Great Opportunities? The Person You Haven't Met Yet," organizational psychologist Tanya Menon explains that doing so can expand our opportunities in ways we often underestimate.

Menon recalls a famous paper by sociologist Mark Granovetter, in which he asked people how they got their jobs. "And what he learned was that most people don't get their jobs through their strong ties—their father, their mother, their significant other," she explains. "They instead get jobs through weak ties—people who they just met."

So how do you establish these "weak ties"? The answer may be a little surprising. "Find the most irritating person you see . . . and connect with them," says Menon. "What you are doing with this exercise is you are forcing yourself to see what you don't want to see, to connect with who you don't want to connect with, to widen your social world."

We have to fight our tendency to go for the easy choices. For example, when Menon is teaching, she doesn't let her students sit in the same seats, week on week. "I move them around from seat to seat. I force them to work with different people so there are more accidental bumps in the network."

Could pursuing such "accidental bumps" lead to new opportunities as a creative? Well, you'll only know if you try.

Q FIND OUT MORE

Tanya Menon's talk:
"The Secret to Great Opportunities? The Person You Haven't Met Yet"
2017

Also try Kare Anderson's talk:
"Be an Opportunity Maker"
2014

IMPROVE YOUR GLOBAL UNDERSTANDING

"Bridge figures" help you escape your comfort zone.

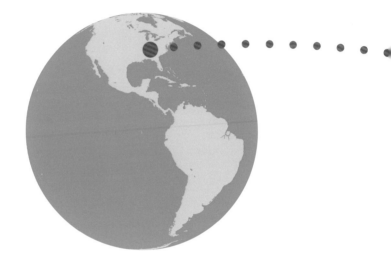

 Online, just like in "real life," most of us end up talking mainly to people just like ourselves. As blogger and technologist Ethan Zuckerman says in his talk "Listening to Global Voices," "If you are like me, a big, geeky white American guy, you tend to interact with a lot of other geeky white American guys. And you don't necessarily have the sense that Twitter is, in fact, a very heavily Brazilian space. It's also—extremely surprising to many Americans—a heavily African American space."

But when differences in language, culture, and personal experience stand in the way, how do we expand our online social network beyond people just like ourselves? One way is to look for what Zuckerman calls "bridge figures." He gives the example of Erik Hersman, telling the audience, "He goes by the moniker 'White African.' He's both a very well known American geek, but he's also Kenyan; he was born in Sudan, grew up in Kenya."

Hersman is a bridge figure, says Zuckerman, because he's "someone who literally has feet in both worlds: one in the

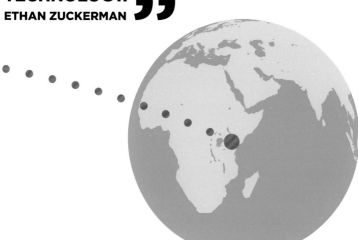

"HE'S ABLE TO TELL A STORY ABOUT THIS BLACKSMITH IN KIBERA AND TURN IT INTO A STORY ABOUT REPURPOSING TECHNOLOGY. "

ETHAN ZUCKERMAN

world of the African technology community, one in the world of the American technology community. And so he's able to tell a story about this blacksmith in Kibera and turn it into a story about repurposing technology."

In short, "He knows one world, and he's finding a way to communicate it to another world, both of which he has deep connections to." Ask yourself: Who might the bridge figures in your area of creativity be? Also turn to page 106 to learn more about how diversity can boost creativity.

Q FIND OUT MORE

Ethan Zuckerman's talk:
"Listening to Global Voices"
2010

Also try Dave Isay's talk:
"Everyone Around You Has a Story the World Needs to Hear"
2015

COLLABORATE ON A MASSIVE SCALE

Don't just work with a few people; work with millions!

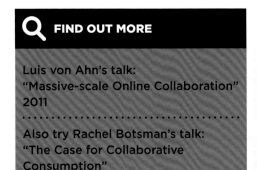

It's nice to work by yourself, or in a small team. But as computer scientist Luis von Ahn points out in his talk "Massive-scale Online Collaboration," greater numbers can lead to greater results.

"If you look at humanity's large-scale achievements, these really big things that humanity has gotten together and done historically—like, for example, building the pyramids of Egypt or the Panama Canal or putting a man on the Moon—there is a curious fact about them," he says. "They were all done with about 100,000 people."

Of course, until recently coordinating such numbers was something only governments or corporate leaders could do. But the internet has changed all that. Now we can all potentially do it, and the people helping us might not even know they're doing so!

As an example, von Ahn explains how his reCAPTCHA project has helped to digitize the world's books. CAPTCHAs are little puzzles that many websites present their visitors, to make sure they are really humans and not bots. The reCAPTCHA project engineered these puzzles so that humans could help solve a problem that software alone couldn't: translating the ornately styled letters of old books into digitized text.

"I've just shown you a project where we've gotten 750 million people to help us digitize human knowledge," von Ahn concludes. "So the question that motivates my research is, if we can put a man on the Moon with 100,000, what can we do with 100 million?"

🔍 FIND OUT MORE

Luis von Ahn's talk:
"Massive-scale Online Collaboration"
2011

Also try Rachel Botsman's talk:
"The Case for Collaborative Consumption"
2010

WE'VE GOTTEN 750 MILLION PEOPLE TO HELP US DIGITIZE HUMAN KNOWLEDGE.

LUIS VON AHN

LEARN TO SPEAK UP FOR YOURSELF

How to advocate for your own interests.

To collaborate successfully, we have to learn to advocate for ourselves. If not, we might end up letting the other people on the project walk all over us. In his talk "How to Speak Up for Yourself," social psychologist Adam Galinsky explains one of the most important tools we have for doing this, which he calls perspective-taking.

"Perspective-taking is really simple," says Galinsky. "It's simply looking at the world through the eyes of another person . . . When I take your perspective, and I think about what you really want, you're more likely to give me what I really want."

He gives an example that sounds like a tall story, but really did happen. In 2010, a 59-year-old man walked into a bank in Watsonville, California, and told workers he had a bomb in his backpack. He threatened to detonate it unless he was given $2,000.

"Now, the bank manager didn't give him the money," explains Galinsky. "She took a step back. She took his perspective, and she noticed something really important. He asked for a specific amount of money. So she said, 'Why did you ask for $2,000?'

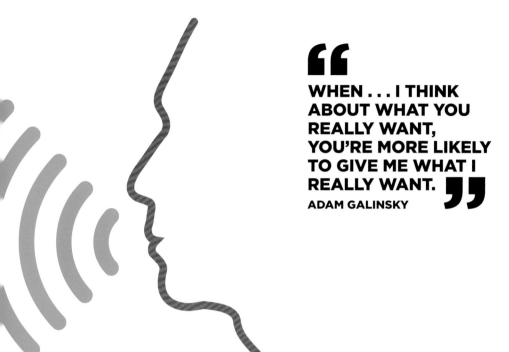

> **WHEN . . . I THINK ABOUT WHAT YOU REALLY WANT, YOU'RE MORE LIKELY TO GIVE ME WHAT I REALLY WANT.**
>
> **ADAM GALINSKY**

"He said, 'My friend is going to be evicted unless I get him $2,000 immediately.' And she said, 'Oh! You don't want to rob the bank, you want to take out a loan. Why don't you come back to my office, and we can have you fill out the paperwork?'"

It didn't end well for the man, who was arrested while completing the forms. But it's an excellent, if offbeat, example of how seeing the other person's perspective can help you stand your ground and stick up for yourself in a work situation. For more on boosting your confidence, turn to page 116.

🔍 FIND OUT MORE

Adam Galinsky's talk:
"How to Speak Up for Yourself"
2016

Also try David Kelley's talk:
"How to Build Your Creative Confidence"
2012

CRAFT BETTER CONVERSATIONS ONLINE

Depart the echo chamber and think back to kindergarten.

We've all fallen prey to the "echo chamber," in which we surround ourselves with people who think the same as us, and forget that other people in wider society have different views. This doesn't just lead to polarized politics. In your creative work, you can be fooled into thinking the whole world likes a particular type of typography, or listens to a certain style of music, just because the people in your social networks do.

In their talk "Free Yourself from Your Filter Bubbles," domestic peace advocate Joan Blades and technologist John Gable explain that to solve this problem you have to add diversity to your networks. "Not just racial and gender," adds Gable, "but also . . . diversity of age, like young and old; rural and urban; liberal and conservative."

We also have to learn to talk online in a more measured way. We need to avoid the kinds of schoolyard fights that typically take place on social media, and instead pursue what Blades calls "living room conversations."

These are, she explains, "simple conversations where two friends with different viewpoints each invite two friends

> **THIS IS A DEEP LISTENING PRACTICE; IT'S NEVER A DEBATE. AND THAT'S INCREDIBLY POWERFUL.**
> **JOAN BLADES**

for structured conversation, where everyone's agreed to some simple ground rules: curiosity, listening, respect, taking turns. Everything we learned in kindergarten, right? Really easy."

And Blades stresses one more thing: "This is a deep listening practice; it's never a debate. And that's incredibly powerful. These conversations in our own living rooms, with people who have different viewpoints, are an incredible adventure."

It might sound like a tall order in our fast-paced digital world. But hey, if we could do this in kindergarten, we can do it now—right?

Q FIND OUT MORE

Joan Blades and John Gable's talk: "Free Yourself from Your Filter Bubbles"
2017

Also try Erica Joy Baker's talk: "How Do We Bridge the Anxiety Gap at Work?"
2017

DIVERSITY BOOSTS CREATIVITY

Fact: diverse companies are more innovative.

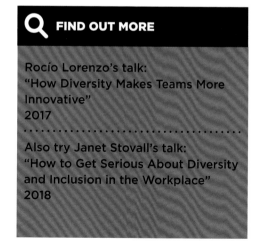

Are diverse companies really more innovative? Management consultant Rocío Lorenzo surveyed 171 companies in Germany, Austria, and Switzerland to find out. And the answer was a clear yes.

In her talk "How Diversity Makes Teams More Innovative," Lorenzo explains that the survey asked companies two things: how innovative they are, and how diverse they are. To measure the first, they were asked about innovation revenue: the share of revenues they'd made from new products and services over the previous three years.

In other words, the researchers weren't interested in how *many* creative ideas companies had (that wouldn't have taken into account the quality of ideas), but whether ideas had translated into products and services that had made them more successful. To measure diversity, meanwhile, the researchers looked at six different factors, including country of origin, age, and gender.

"A couple of months later, the data came in, and the results convinced the most skeptical among us," enthuses Lorenzo. "The answer was a clear yes. No ifs, no buts. The data in our sample showed that more diverse companies are simply more innovative, period."

So whether you're recruiting for a business or looking for collaborators on a one-off project, the message is the same. Don't automatically look for people who are just like you. Instead, strive for diversity, and you're likely to get a real and measurable payoff in terms of innovation.

Q FIND OUT MORE

Rocío Lorenzo's talk:
"How Diversity Makes Teams More Innovative"
2017

Also try Janet Stovall's talk:
"How to Get Serious About Diversity and Inclusion in the Workplace"
2018

HOW TO DEAL WITH AN IMPASSE

Being prepared to be wrong is a strength, not a weakness.

One of the most frustrating parts of collaborating with another creative is when both of you "know" that you're right about something, and neither will back down.

We know in theory that everyone makes mistakes, but we're loathe to admit that we ever do so ourselves. In her talk "On Being Wrong," writer and author Kathryn Schulz points out that, as a consequence, "we all kind of wind up traveling through life, trapped in this little bubble of feeling very right about everything."

This can prove disastrous for any kind of collaboration. As Schulz says, "The first thing we usually do when someone disagrees with us is we just assume they're ignorant. They don't have access to the same information that we do, and when we generously share that information with them, they're going to see the light."

If that doesn't work, we move on to other assumptions: "that they're idiots" or "they know the truth, and they are deliberately distorting it."

Of course, if we want to move past a disagreement and work successfully with others, we need to end this vicious circle. Or, as Schulz puts it, "You need to step outside of that tiny, terrified space of rightness and look around at each other, and look out at the vastness and complexity and mystery of the universe, and be able to say, 'Wow, I don't know. Maybe I'm wrong.'"

Try it. It might sound scary, but it can be quite liberating!

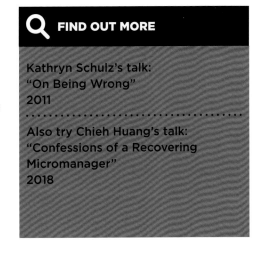

Q FIND OUT MORE

Kathryn Schulz's talk:
"On Being Wrong"
2011
. . . .
Also try Chieh Huang's talk:
"Confessions of a Recovering Micromanager"
2018

YOU NEED TO STEP OUTSIDE OF THAT TINY, TERRIFIED SPACE OF RIGHTNESS AND LOOK AROUND AT EACH OTHER.

KATHRYN SCHULZ

HOW TO ARGUE EFFECTIVELY

Structured debate is more productive than grandstanding.

Communication via the internet is instant and easy. But when it comes to arguing a point, it encourages us to be rigid and stand our ground, which makes resolution very difficult.

Julia Dhar has a background as a world debate champion. In her talk "How to Disagree Productively and Find Common Ground," she argues that debating a point of disagreement in person, and in a structured manner, is usually much more effective.

"Debate requires that we engage with the conflicting idea, directly, respectfully, face to face," she explains. "The foundation of debate is rebuttal—the idea that you make a claim and I provide a response, and you respond to my response. Without rebuttal, it's not debate, it's just pontificating."

And debate is much easier face to face. Dhar points to research by Professor Juliana Schroeder and her team at the University of California, Berkeley, which suggests that listening to someone's voice as they make a controversial argument is "literally humanizing; it makes it easier to engage with what that person has to say."

Dhar's conclusion is clear. "Step away from the keyboards; start conversing," she urges. "And if we are to expand that notion a little bit, nothing is stopping us from pressing pause on a parade of keynote speeches, the sequence of very polite panel discussions, and replacing some of that with a structured debate."

Whether you're looking to solve the world's problems, or just agree on the direction of a creative project, this seems like good advice to follow.

FIND OUT MORE

Julia Dhar's talk:
"How to Disagree Productively and Find Common Ground"
2018

Also try Cal Newport's talk:
"Why You Should Quit Social Media"
2016

"STEP AWAY FROM THE KEYBOARDS; START CONVERSING."

JULIA DHAR

COLLABORATE WITH YOUR AUDIENCE

How to get viewers involved in the creative process.

When we think about collaborating with others, it's usually other creatives who spring to mind. But what about collaborating with your audience?

In her talk "An Art Made of Trust, Vulnerability, and Connection," Marina Abramović explains that in performance art, the audience is as integral to the work as its creator. "Energy dialog happens; the audience and the performer make the piece together," she explains.

Abramović describes her performance at New York's Museum of Modern Art, where she sat in a chair at a table with another vacant chair opposite. People were encouraged to sit in the empty chair and face her, for as long as they wanted.

"The curator said to me, 'That's ridiculous! You know, this is New York. This chair will be empty, nobody has time,'" Abramović recalls. But as she sat there eight to ten hours a day, over the course of three months, the public did indeed respond, and actively took part in the way she'd hoped.

"They would come and sit in front of me," she recalls. "There was so much pain and loneliness. So many incredible things when you look in somebody else's eyes. Because in the gaze with that total stranger, during which you never even say one word, everything happened."

And the experience made a lasting impression on her. "I understood when I stood up from that chair after three months, I am not the same anymore. And I understood that I have a very strong mission: that I have to communicate this experience to everybody."

You don't have to be a performance artist to be inspired by Abramović's story. If people like something cultural, they love having the opportunity to become part of the experience, whether it's an artwork, a TV show, a website, or anything else. So why not try to think of ways to help them do so?

Q FIND OUT MORE

Marina Abramović's talk:
"An Art Made of Trust, Vulnerability,
and Connection"
2015

Also try Amanda Palmer's talk:
"The Art of Asking"
2013

"

**IN THE GAZE WITH
THAT TOTAL STRANGER,
DURING WHICH YOU
NEVER EVEN SAY ONE
WORD, EVERYTHING
HAPPENED.** "
MARINA ABRAMOVIĆ

BE INNOVATIVE
and try new ways of working

In a rapidly changing world, we can no longer rely on the old ways. This chapter examines some new and potentially game-changing approaches to work.

BECOME IMMUNE TO REJECTION

Desensitize yourself, and you'll soon feel liberated.

Rejection sucks, but you can actually desensitize yourself to it. In his talk "What I Learned from 100 Days of Rejection," author, blogger, and entrepreneur Jia Jiang explains how he did just that, video-blogging his experiences along the way.

On day one, he began by asking a total stranger for $100. "And he looked up, he's like, 'No. Why?' And I just said, 'No? I'm sorry.' Then I turned around, and I just ran. I felt so embarrassed."

On day two, he went to a burger joint, ate a burger, and then asked the staff for a "burger refill." Predictably, he was rejected again by a bemused employee. "But the life-and-death feeling I was feeling the first time was no longer there, just because I stayed engaged, because I didn't run. I said, 'Wow! Great, I'm already learning things. Great!' "

On day three, Jiang went to a Krispy Kreme and asked them to interlink five doughnuts together to form the Olympic rings. To his surprise, the staff obliged, and the resulting video got 5 million views on YouTube.

The experiment continued, and by the end of the 100 days, Jiang's perspective on life had completely changed. "Rejection was my curse, was my boogeyman," he explains. "It has bothered me my whole life because I was running away from it. [When] I started embracing it, I turned that into the biggest gift in my life."

Q FIND OUT MORE

Jia Jiang's talk:
"What I Learned from 100 Days of Rejection"
2015

Also try Alison Ledgerwood's talk:
"A Simple Trick to Improve Positive Thinking"
2013

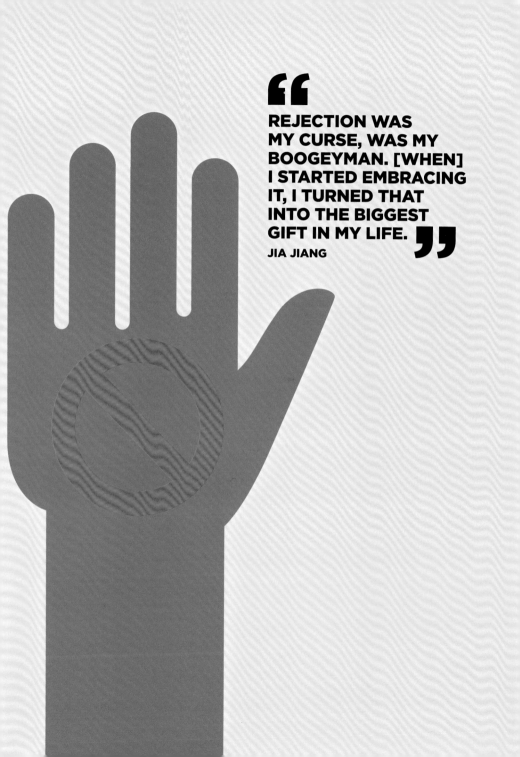

"REJECTION WAS MY CURSE, WAS MY BOOGEYMAN. [WHEN] I STARTED EMBRACING IT, I TURNED THAT INTO THE BIGGEST GIFT IN MY LIFE."

JIA JIANG

LEARN TO EMBRACE SMALL RISKS

Embracing minor perils can have a major career impact.

Only the very brave or very foolhardy take big risks with their lives and careers. But small risks that get you out of your comfort zone? Those are exactly what we need to take, says educator Tina Seelig.

In her talk "The Little Risks You Can Take to Increase Your Luck," Seelig gives an example. "I was on an airplane, early, early morning flight on my way to Ecuador," she recalls. "Normally, I'd just put on my headphones and go to sleep, wake up, do some work. But I decided to take a little risk, and I started a conversation with the man sitting next to me."

He turned out to be a publisher, and they started chatting. About three-quarters of the way through the flight, she took another risk, sharing a book proposal with him.

She got a "thanks, but no thanks," but they exchanged details and a couple of months later he agreed to come to her writing class. After a long, somewhat circuitous sequence of events, Seelig ultimately ended up getting her original proposal accepted, not by him but by one of his colleagues.

Within two years, that book had sold over a million copies around the world. "Now, you might say, 'Oh, you're so lucky,'" concludes Seelig. "But that luck resulted from a series of small risks I took, starting with saying hello. And anyone can do this."

Q FIND OUT MORE

Tina Seelig's talk:
"The Little Risks You Can Take to Increase Your Luck"
2018

Also try Siawn Ou's talk:
"The Art of Letting Go . . . of the Floor"
2015

HOW TO CELEBRATE YOUR FAILURES

Aiming to fail is more efficient than trying to succeed.

It's natural when we make a mistake in our creative work to hide it from others, or even from ourselves. But in his talk "The Unexpected Benefit of Celebrating Failure," author and technologist Astro Teller argues that we should do the very opposite, and actually celebrate it.

This approach has worked well, he says, at Google X (now X Developments), a "moonshot factory" that aims to provide radical solutions to the world's biggest problems, such as balloons that provide free internet to the developing world.

Celebrating failure was necessary, says Teller, because "being audacious and working on big, risky things makes people inherently uncomfortable. They worry. 'What will happen to me if I fail? Will people laugh at me? Will I be fired?'"

Consequently, the only way to get people at Google X to experiment and think outside the box properly was to turn that on its head, and make failure a cause for celebration.

What that means in practice, says Teller, is that "teams kill their ideas as soon as the evidence is on the table because they're rewarded for it. They get applause from their peers. Hugs and high fives from their manager—me in particular. They get promoted for it. We have bonused every single person on teams that ended their projects, from teams as small as two to teams of more than thirty."

It might sound weird. But if one of the world's biggest companies can celebrate its own creative failures, shouldn't you consider doing so with your own?

Q FIND OUT MORE

Astro Teller's talk:
"The Unexpected Benefit of Celebrating Failure"
2016

Also try Raphael Rose's talk:
"How Failure Cultivates Resilience"
2018

HOW TO AVOID BEATING YOURSELF UP

Remember that creativity is about reaching, not arriving.

Typically, talks about being creatively successful are all about winning. But in her talk "Embrace the Near Win," art historian and critic Sarah Lewis takes a different approach.

During her first museum job, Lewis noticed something important about the artist Elizabeth Murray, for whom she was preparing a retrospective: not every artwork was a total masterpiece. She went on to ask Murray what she thought of her early works, and learned that some hadn't met the mark and had been thrown into the trash. In that moment, Lewis's view of success and creativity spun on its axis, and she realized that "mastery is in the reaching, not the arriving."

In other words, it's not about the end goal. Instead, it's about "constantly wanting to close that gap between where you are and where you want to be," says Lewis. "It's a wisdom understood by Duke Ellington, who said that his favorite song out of his repertoire was always the next one."

So, don't ever beat yourself up because your creative work isn't perfect. In short, it probably never will be and nor, to be frank, will anyone else's. But it's the series of near wins along the way to your dream that are the things truly worth living for.

Q FIND OUT MORE

Sarah Lewis's talk:
"Embrace the Near Win"
2014
....
Also try Charly Haversat's talk:
"Perfectionism Holds Us Back.
Here's Why"
2015

"

MASTERY IS IN THE REACHING, NOT THE ARRIVING. **"**

SARAH LEWIS

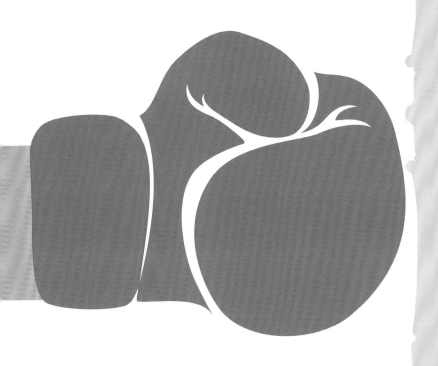

DESIGN FOR ALL FIVE SENSES

New tech enables us to engage audiences in novel ways.

We typically think about creative work applying to one, or at most two, of the senses. Musicians target our ears; artists our eyes. But how about targeting all five?

As Christel Beltran points out in her talk "Design for All Five Senses," modern technology is getting so advanced that "soon, computers will be able to breathe, feel, hear, see, move, and even have enhanced capabilities compared to our own senses." So, it's worth thinking of ways to take advantage of these new capabilities.

Touch, for example, can be represented by electric impulses that our fingers, our nerve endings, send to our brains when we feel things in the world around us. "Soon, we will be able to use these signals to create digital models of the materials that we touch, so that the information can be learned by computers," Beltran explains.

This means that we'll be able to reproduce these sensations—perhaps via vibrations on our mobile phones. And it would allow consumers, for example, to get a sense of what things feel like to the touch, before they buy them online.

While Beltran's talk focuses mainly on the medical benefits of this emerging tech, it's clearly relevant to creatives. Imagine a song you could smell, or book illustrations you could feel. What other ways might we find to engage our audience's senses more fully?

> **SOON, COMPUTERS WILL BE ABLE TO BREATHE, FEEL, HEAR, SEE, MOVE, AND EVEN HAVE ENHANCED CAPABILITIES COMPARED TO OUR OWN SENSES.**
> **CHRISTEL BELTRAN**

Q FIND OUT MORE

Christel Beltran's talk:
"Design for All Five Senses"
2013

Also try David Eagleman's talk:
"Can We Create New Senses for Humans?"
2015

64/100
LEAVE THE OFFICE TO BE MORE PRODUCTIVE

The office is an outdated concept. It's time to work elsewhere.

Software entrepreneur Jason Fried has a radical theory: that the office isn't a good place to work. In his talk "Why Work Doesn't Happen at Work," he admits that this is not the standard view. But he says the received wisdom is now totally out of date.

For more than ten years, Fried has been asking people, "'Where do you really want to go when you really need to get something done?' I'll hear things like the porch, the deck, the kitchen. I'll hear things like an extra room in the house, the basement, the coffee shop, the library. And then you'll hear things like the train, a plane, a car—so, the commute."

In short, people almost never say "the office," and that's not surprising. Because "what you find is that, especially with creative people—designers, programmers, writers, engineers, thinkers—that people really need long stretches of uninterrupted time to get something done." Yet the office is full of constant interruptions, so that almost never happens.

If you really want to be creative, maybe consider spending less time at the office and more time working from home. Or if that's not possible, find ways to reduce the number of distractions at the office itself. As Fried suggests, "We've all heard of the 'casual Friday' thing . . . But how about 'no-talk Thursdays'?"

FIND OUT MORE

Jason Fried's talk: "Why Work Doesn't Happen at Work" 2010

Also try Matt Mullenweg's talk: "Why Working from Home Is Good for Business" 2019

"
CREATIVE PEOPLE . . . REALLY
NEED LONG STRETCHES OF
UNINTERRUPTED TIME TO GET
SOMETHING DONE. "
JASON FRIED

BOOST CREATIVITY THROUGH SLEEP

Better sleep will make you more inspired and productive.

Traditionally, common wisdom said that the way to be more successful at work was to work more and sleep less. But Arianna Huffington, cofounder and former editor in chief of the *Huffington Post*, believes that's counterproductive. And in her talk "How to Succeed? Get More Sleep," she explains how it's a subject that's close to her heart.

"I learned the hard way the value of sleep," she reveals. "Two and a half years ago, I fainted from exhaustion. I hit my head on my desk. I broke my cheekbone, I got five stitches on my right eye. And I began the journey of rediscovering the value of sleep."

In the course of this journey, Huffington studied, met with doctors and scientists, and gradually came to the conclusion that "the way to a more productive, more inspired, more joyful life is getting enough sleep."

It's important to stick to your guns, though, she adds, because the current culture is working in the opposite direction and encouraging sleep deprivation. "Especially here in Washington. If you try to make a breakfast date, and you say, 'How about eight o'clock?' they're likely to tell you, 'Eight o'clock is too late for me. But that's OK, I can get a game of tennis in and do a few conference calls and meet you at eight.'"

$z_z z^z z^{z z}z^{z z}z^z z_z z$

> ## "
> **THE WAY TO A MORE PRODUCTIVE, MORE INSPIRED, MORE JOYFUL LIFE IS GETTING ENOUGH SLEEP.**
> **ARIANNA HUFFINGTON** "

When they say such things, people think they're conveying an image that they're incredibly busy and productive. "But the truth is, they're not, because we, at the moment, have had brilliant leaders in business, in finance, in politics, making terrible decisions," says Huffington. She concludes, "I urge you to shut your eyes, and discover the great ideas that lie inside us; to shut your engines and discover the power of sleep."

Q FIND OUT MORE

Arianna Huffington's talk:
"How to Succeed? Get More Sleep"
2010

. . . .

Also try Matt Walker's talk:
"Sleep Is Your Superpower"
2019

PRACTICE EMOTIONAL FIRST AID

Prioritizing mental health makes us happier and more fulfilled.

We'd all go to the doctor if we had a workplace injury. So why, when we suffer emotional pain such as guilt, loss, or loneliness, do we rarely do anything at all?

That's the question psychologist and author Guy Winch poses in his talk "Why We All Need to Practice Emotional First Aid." He points out, "Even though there are scientifically proven techniques we could use to treat these kinds of psychological injuries, we don't."

For instance, we all need to start identifying our most unhealthy psychological habits. "One of the most common is called rumination, which means to chew over," says Winch. "It's when your boss yells at you . . . and you just can't stop replaying the scene in your head for days, sometimes for weeks on end." But in

developing such a habit, "you are actually putting yourself at significant risk for developing clinical depression, alcoholism, eating disorders, and even cardiovascular disease."

If we address these problems head on, says Winch, we can create a world where people are happier and more fulfilled. "That's the world I want to live in," he says. "And if you just become informed and change a few simple habits, well, that's the world we can all live in."

FIND OUT MORE

Guy Winch's talk:
"Why We All Need to Practice Emotional First Aid"
2014

Also try Sangu Delle's talk:
"There's No Shame in Taking Care of Your Mental Health"
2017

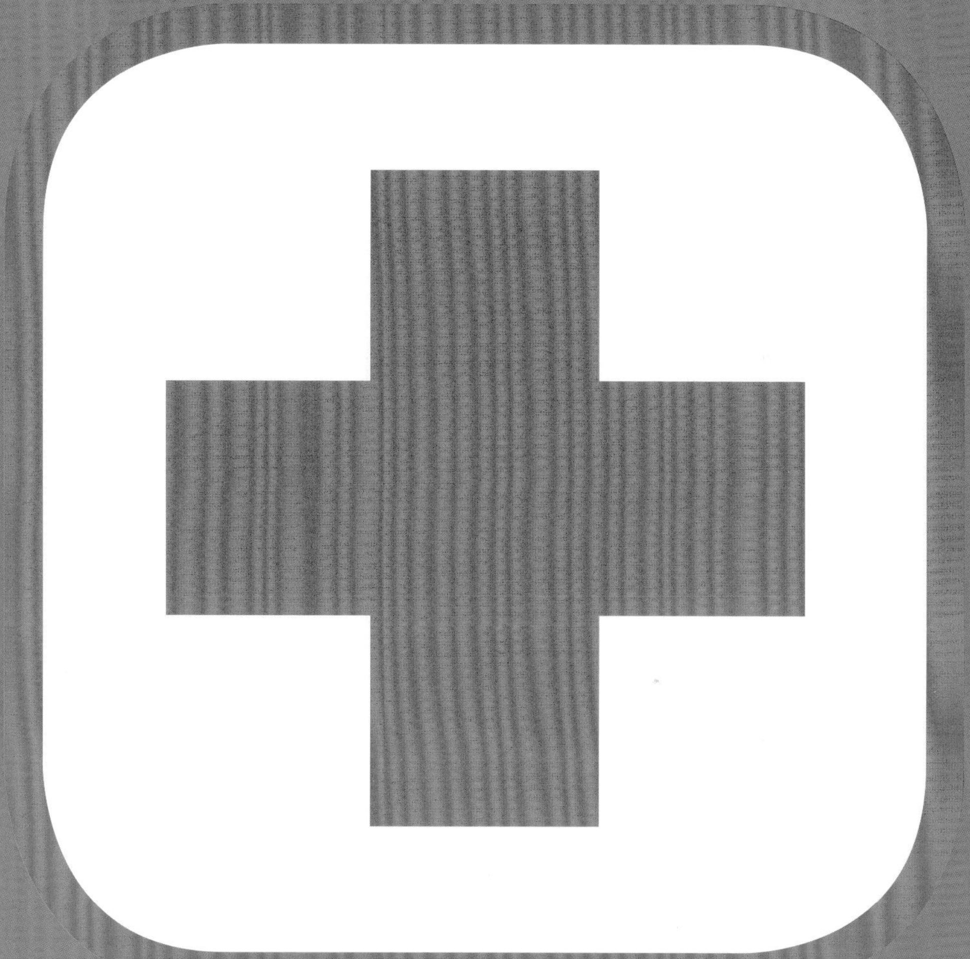

WHY HAPPINESS MAKES YOU MORE PRODUCTIVE

Productivity follows happiness, not the other way around.

Most of us think we need to work harder in order to be happy. But according to Shawn Achor, psychologist and founder of the consultancy Good Think Inc., that's actually the wrong way around. In fact, he argues, happiness inspires us to be more productive.

"If you can raise somebody's level of positivity in the present, then their brain experiences what we now call a happiness advantage," he explains. "Your intelligence rises, your creativity rises, your energy levels rise. In fact, we've found that every single business outcome improves. Your brain at 'positive' is thirty-one percent more productive than your brain at negative, neutral, or stressed."

So, how do you become happier in practice? In his talk, "The Happy Secret to Better Work," Achor offers a series of suggestions. "Journaling about one positive experience you've had over the past twenty-four hours allows your brain to relive it," he says. "Exercise teaches your brain that your behavior matters. Meditation allows your brain to get over the cultural ADHD that we've been creating by trying to do multiple tasks at once, and allows our brains to focus on the task at hand."

Finally, Achor recommends random acts of kindness. For example, whenever you open your inbox, write one positive email praising or thanking somebody in your support network. "By doing these activities and by training your brain just like we train our bodies, what we've found is we can reverse the formula for happiness and success, and in doing so, not only create ripples of positivity, but a real revolution," he says.

FIND OUT MORE

Shawn Achor's talk:
"The Happy Secret to Better Work"
2011

Also try Michael C. Bush's talk:
"This Is What Makes Employees Happy at Work"
2018

FREE UP TIME BY SAYING NO TO MEETINGS

Stop saying yes to meetings automatically, and reduce stress.

Very few creative people like meetings or find them useful, so why do we say yes to so many of them? Information security manager David Grady is on a mission to change all of that.

In his talk "How to Save the World (Or at Least Yourself) from Bad Meetings," he paints a typical picture. "It's Tuesday morning and you're at the office, and a meeting invitation pops up in your calendar. And it's from this woman who you kind of know from down the hall, and the subject line references some project that you heard a little bit about.

"But there's no agenda. There's no information about why you were invited to the meeting. And yet you accept the meeting invitation, and you go."

When this futile and pointless endeavor concludes, you go back to your desk and say, "Boy, I wish I had those two hours back." So why do we never learn from such experiences?

We wouldn't let a colleague steal our office chair, Grady reasons, so why do we let them steal our time? Instead of blindly accepting meeting invites, he urges, we should first push for a full explanation of why the meeting is necessary.

"If we do this often enough, and we do it respectfully, people might start to be a little bit more thoughtful . . . and you can make more thoughtful decisions about accepting it. People might actually start sending out agendas. Imagine!"

🔍 FIND OUT MORE

David Grady's talk:
"How to Save the World (Or at Least Yourself) from Bad Meetings"
2013

Also try Laura Vanderkam's talk:
"How to Gain Control of Your Free Time"
2016

WHY TO TAKE A YEAR OFF FROM WORK

It's not just students who should take a gap year.

Want to really reenergize your creativity muscles? How about taking a year off? If that sounds impractical, then bear in mind that one of the world's most renowned creatives, Austrian-born designer Stefan Sagmeister, closes down his New York studio for twelve months every seven years.

As he points out in his talk "The Power of Time Off," most people expect to spend at least fifteen years in retirement. So why not slice five of these years up and bring them forward?

In Sagmeister's case, he doesn't just sit around watching TV during these yearlong sabbaticals, but pursues creative experiments. These have ranged from a movie about happiness in Bali to an art installation in Amsterdam involving 250,000 coins. What connects them is that they're all "things that are always difficult to accomplish during the regular working year."

During these sabbatical years, Sagmeister has also spent time traveling, reading books he'd never otherwise have time for, and renovating his studio. "In that year, we are not available for any of our clients; we are totally closed," he explains. "And as you can imagine, it is a lovely and very energetic time."

Q FIND OUT MORE

Stefan Sagmeister's talk:
"The Power of Time Off"
2009
. . . .
Also try Carol Fishman Cohen's talk:
"How to Get Back to Work After a Career Break"
2015

IN THAT YEAR, WE ARE NOT AVAILABLE FOR ANY OF OUR CLIENTS; WE ARE TOTALLY CLOSED. AND AS YOU CAN IMAGINE, IT IS A LOVELY AND VERY ENERGETIC TIME.

STEFAN SAGMEISTER

BE SUCCESSFUL
as a creative

In today's world, success is not always about being the biggest or best, but finding a niche and engaging with an audience on a profound and sustainable level.

BE A SUCCESS BY PLAYING THE LONG GAME

Success requires continuous energy and passion.

> **WE FIGURE WE'VE MADE IT, WE SIT BACK IN OUR COMFORT ZONE, AND WE ACTUALLY STOP DOING EVERYTHING THAT MADE US SUCCESSFUL.**
>
> **RICHARD ST. JOHN**

Why do so many people veer between success and failure? According to marketer Richard St. John, it's because we've got the wrong idea of what success actually means.

"We think success is a one-way street," he explains in his talk "Success Is a Continuous Journey." "So we do everything that leads up to success, but then we get there. We figure we've made it, we sit back in our comfort zone, and we actually stop doing everything that made us successful. And it doesn't take long to go downhill."

St. John knows this to be fact, because it happened to him. "[To reach] success, I worked hard, I pushed myself," he explains. "But then I stopped, because I figured, 'Oh, you know, I made it. I can just sit back and relax.'"

At this point, he stopped focusing on clients and projects, and got distracted by all the money flowing in. "Suddenly, I was on the phone to my stockbroker and my real estate agent, when I should have been talking to my clients . . . Then I got into stuff that I didn't love, like management. I am the world's worst manager, but I figured I should be doing it, because I was, after all, the president of the company."

Eventually, St. John gave up trying, lost focus, became depressed, and was put on

antidepressants by his doctor. "It didn't take long for business to drop like a rock. My partner and I . . . had to let all our employees go. It was down to just the two of us, and we were about to go under."

Ultimately, St. John pulled things back and the business became more successful than ever. And he learned a valuable lesson: that you cannot rest on your laurels. Because success is not a "one and done" deal but something that requires continuous energy and commitment.

🔍 FIND OUT MORE

Richard St. John's talk:
"Success Is a Continuous Journey"
2009

. . . .

Also try Richard St. John's talk:
"Eight Secrets of Success"
2005

DEFINE WHAT SUCCESS MEANS FOR YOU

Don't let your ambitions be governed by norms.

We all *think* we know what success looks like. But are we correct? In his talk "A Kinder, Gentler Philosophy of Success," philosopher and author Alain de Botton argues that our visions of success are usually defined not by us as individuals, but by others.

For example, "When we're told that banking is a very respectable profession, a lot of us want to go into banking. When banking is no longer so respectable, we lose interest in banking. We are highly open to suggestion."

Even material things, de Botton argues, aren't what we truly want; it's more about what they represent to others. "The next time you see somebody driving a Ferrari, don't think, 'This is somebody who's greedy,'" he says. "Think, 'This is somebody who is incredibly vulnerable and in need of love.'"

His conclusion? "We should focus in on our ideas, and make sure that we own them; that we are truly the authors of our own ambitions." As de Botton stresses, "It's bad enough not getting what you want. But it's even worse to [find out] it isn't, in fact, what you wanted all along."

So, stop thinking of success in terms of the usual clichés—money, fame, power, status—and instead consider what you truly want, deep down. That might mean, for example, creating art you're proud of, whether or not it sells. After all, Vincent Van Gogh is said to have sold only one painting in his life, but no one would ever say his career wasn't a success!

Q FIND OUT MORE

Alain de Botton's talk:
"A Kinder, Gentler Philosophy of Success"
2009

Also try John Wooden's talk:
"The Difference Between Winning and Succeeding"
2001

WE SHOULD FOCUS IN ON OUR IDEAS, AND MAKE SURE THAT WE OWN THEM; THAT WE ARE TRULY THE AUTHORS OF OUR OWN AMBITIONS.

ALAIN DE BOTTON

HOW TO FEEL A SENSE OF CONTROL

Being a success is something that comes from inside.

Success, believes advertising guru Rory Sutherland, is mainly a question of perspective. As he points out in his talk "Perspective Is Everything," a person standing alone with a drink at a party might be seen as a sad loner. But someone staring out the window and smoking a cigarette might be seen as a "cool philosopher." It's all about framing.

"What we have is exactly the same thing, the same activity," he explains. "But one of them makes you feel great and the other one, with just a small change of posture, makes you feel terrible." Sutherland also notes how England's middle classes have rebranded unemployment as a gap year. "Because having a son who's unemployed in Manchester is really quite embarrassing. But having a son who's unemployed in Thailand is really viewed as quite an accomplishment."

Overall, what's more important than our actual circumstances is feeling a sense of control over them. And so the power to rebrand ourselves is crucial, whether that's from an "unpopular" artist to a "genre-defying, experimental" one, or a "victim of redundancy" to an "independent freelancer."

As Sutherland says, "The power to rebrand things—to understand that our experiences, costs, things don't actually much depend on what they really are, but on how we view them . . . I genuinely think can't be overstated."

As we learned in Shawn Achor's talk "The Happy Secret to Better Work" (see page 130), productivity follows happiness, not the other way around. So is it time you rebranded yourself, to make you feel you have more control over your life?

Q FIND OUT MORE

Rory Sutherland's talk:
"Perspective Is Everything"
2011

Also try Chip Conley's talk:
"Measuring What Makes Life Worthwhile"
2010

VISUALIZE YOUR FEARS

Confronting your worries head on is the best way to tame them.

When you're trying to decide whether to, say, launch a new business or learn a different creative skill, how do you overcome your fear of failure?

In his talk "Turning Fear into Fuel," entrepreneur and author Jonathan Fields suggests that visualization can be a useful technique.

He recommends you start by asking yourself, "What if I failed?" But don't just answer in your own head. "Write it out. Paint a picture. Make it a movie. Make it as vivid as you can."

Once you've done that, the next stage is to ask yourself, "How will I recover?" And this is just as important. "Give equal attention to that picture," Fields stresses. "Plot out exactly what you will do to get yourself back. What most people find is, doing that alone goes a long way toward disempowering the fear of failure, because they realize almost everything is recoverable. It may suck a little bit, it may be hard, but it's recoverable."

Finally, Fields urges you to ask yourself, "What if I do nothing?" How will that impact your life? "If you're a little bit unhappy now, do you think ten, twenty, thirty years of doing nothing will keep you a little bit unhappy now?" he questions. If you can be truly honest with your answer, you'll soon know whether or not to go ahead with your plans.

You can find more advice about facing your fears in David Kelley's talk on guided mastery (see page 23) and Astro Teller's talk on how to celebrate your failures (see page 119).

Q FIND OUT MORE

**Jonathan Fields's talk:
"Turning Fear into Fuel"
2010**

**Also try Karen Thompson Walker's talk:
"What Fear Can Teach Us"
2012**

FIND YOUR TRUE PASSION

You'll never succeed at anything if it's just "interesting."

What's the key to a successful career? There are many answers to that question, but there's one thing all the experts agree on: you need to find something you have a real passion for.

In "Why You Will Fail to Have a Great Career," a talk laden with irony, Larry Smith—a professor of economics in Canada—calls out some of the absurd excuses people invent when they fail to pursue their passion. "You're too lazy to do it. It's too hard. You're afraid if you look for your passion and don't find it, you'll feel like you're an idiot." Do any of these sound familiar?

Crucially, Smith points out that there's an important difference between a passion and an interest. "Passion is your greatest love," he explains. "Passion is the thing that will help you create the highest expression of your talent. Passion, interest; it's not the same thing. Are you really going to go to

your sweetie and say, 'Marry me! You're interesting?' Won't happen. Won't happen, and you will die alone."

So how *do* you find your true passion? "You need twenty interests," Smith recommends. "And then one of them, one of them might grab you. One of them might engage you more than anything else, and then you may have found your greatest love, in comparison to all the other things that interest you, and that's what passion is."

Q FIND OUT MORE

Larry Smith's talk:
"Why You Will Fail to Have a Great Career"
2011
....
Also try Angela Lee Duckworth's talk:
"Grit: The Power of Passion and Perseverance"
2013

IGNORE YOUR AGE

You can be a success, no matter how old you are.

If you don't set out on the path to success when you're young, you've blown your chances.

Right? Wrong, says Hungarian-American physicist Albert-László Barabási. In his talk "The Real Relationship Between Your Age and Your Chance of Success," he uses mathematical analysis to prove that the notion that "youth is best" is a complete fallacy.

So where did this myth come from? There's a tendency in science, Barabási notes, to focus on geniuses like Albert Einstein who made big discoveries when they were in their twenties and thirties. But in reality, it's not usually this headline-grabbing minority who make the biggest contributions to the discipline.

And it's the same story with today's Silicon Valley entrepreneurs, Barabási continues. Most of the attention is paid to the young outliers, such as Facebook founder Mark Zuckerberg, who became a billionaire at the age of twenty-four. "[And so] there is this ethos in Silicon Valley that youth equals success."

But when you look at the data and examine exactly who created successful companies and had a successful exit, it turns out that the older you are, the better. "This is so strong," says Barabási, "that if you are in your fifties, you are twice as likely to actually have a successful exit than if you are in your thirties."

In short, the idea that your chance of succeeding reduces with age is just nonsense. So don't be fooled, and take heart in the notion that the longer you pursue your dream, the more likely you are to achieve it.

Q FIND OUT MORE

Albert-László Barabási's talk: "The Real Relationship Between Your Age and Your Chance of Success"
2019

Also try Isabel Allende's talk: "How to Live Passionately—No Matter Your Age"
2014

FIND PEOPLE WHO'LL HELP YOU ADVANCE

Want to get ahead? Find a sponsor.

We often think getting ahead is about doing great work, but executive and author Carla Harris is a great believer in the saying "It's not what you know, but who you know." In her talk "How to Find the Person Who Can Help You Get Ahead at Work," she argues that getting a sponsor is vital.

A sponsor is someone who advocates for you, whether you're applying for a job, asking for a promotion, or seeking funding for a project. Because while we'd all love to be treated purely on the quality of our work, we know deep down that's not how managers make decisions. Realistically, we need someone to make our case—basically, to tell others how great we are.

So how do you get a sponsor? For Harris, it's all about building up what she calls "performance currency" and "relationship currency." The former is about "delivering that which was asked of you and a little bit extra," she says. "Every time you deliver upon an assignment above people's expectations, you generate performance currency."

Relationship currency, meanwhile, is about taking the time "to connect, to engage and to get to know the people that are in your environment, and more importantly to give them the opportunity to know you."

In other words, work hard, but also get to know the people around you. Then, when the time is right, seek out the right person and ask them to be your sponsor. The time you invest in this should pay off handsomely.

FIND OUT MORE

Carla Harris's talk:
"How to Find the Person Who Can Help You Get Ahead at Work"
2018

Also try Lori Hunt's talk:
"The Power of Mentoring"
2013

"

GET TO KNOW THE PEOPLE THAT ARE IN YOUR ENVIRONMENT, AND MORE IMPORTANTLY . . . GIVE THEM THE OPPORTUNITY TO KNOW YOU. "

CARLA HARRIS

HOW TO GO IN THE RIGHT DIRECTION

Be like water, and you'll find your true path.

What's the best path to career success? For IT manager Raymond Tang, it's to ask himself, "What would water do?"

In his talk "Be Humble—and Other Lessons from the Philosophy of Water," Tang explains that when water meets an obstacle, such as a rock, it just flows around it. "It doesn't get upset, it doesn't get angry, it doesn't get agitated. In fact, it doesn't feel much at all. When faced with an obstacle, somehow water finds a solution, without force, without conflict."

Similarly, Tang seeks a calm path in life that does not upset other people or his environment, but works in tandem with them. When he first began taking this approach, he says, "I started asking questions like: 'Will this action bring me greater harmony and bring more harmony to my environment? Does this align with my nature?' . . . I stopped fighting with myself, and I learned to work with my environment to solve its problems."

Tang notes that his organization hosts a lot of hackathons, in which designers try to solve a problem in a short amount of time. And the teams that usually win are not the ones with the most experienced team members but those "who are open to learn, who are open to unlearn, and who are open to helping each other navigate through the changing circumstances."

It's less about fighting to succeed, and more about cooperating to succeed. Could this be the change in attitude you need to turn your career around?

Q FIND OUT MORE

Raymond Tang's talk:
"Be Humble—and Other Lessons from the Philosophy of Water"
2017

Also try Christine Porath's talk:
"Why Being Respectful to Your Coworkers Is Good for Business"
2018

WHY YOU SHOULD STRIVE FOR PERFECTION

Stop aiming for "good enough." You're better than that.

We're all told at school that the important thing is to "try your best." But shouldn't we be aiming higher?

Jon Bowers, who runs a training facility for delivery drivers, certainly thinks so. A hundred people in the United States die every day in car accidents, so for him perfection isn't just an aspiration, it's a must. "In the world of professional driving," he points out, achieving "just 99 percent of the job means somebody dies."

In his talk "We Should Aim for Perfection—and Stop Fearing Failure," Bowers outlines how we can all aim for 100 percent perfection. And the key, somewhat ironically, is being more accepting of our failures.

"Instead of defining perfectionism as a destructive intolerance for failure, why don't we try giving it a new definition?" he argues. "Why don't we try defining perfectionism as a willingness to do what is difficult to achieve? . . . You see, then we can agree that failure is a good thing in our quest for perfection. And when we seek perfection without fear of failure, just think about what we can accomplish."

In other words, by striving for 100 percent perfection but being realistic about your chances of achieving it in the short term, you're far more likely to achieve it in the long term. If we all did that, believes Bowers, "then we could stop fearing failure and we could stop living in a world filled with the consequences of 'good enough.'"

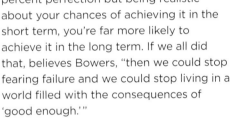

FIND OUT MORE

Jon Bowers's talk:
"We Should Aim for Perfection—and Stop Fearing Failure"
2017

Also try Elizabeth Gilbert's talk:
"Success, Failure and the Drive to Keep Creating"
2014

KEEP YOUR PLANS SECRET

Stay quiet, and you're more likely to achieve your goals.

When we have an exciting plan, whether that be releasing a podcast, starting a creative side project, or launching our own company, it's natural to want to tell people about it. But in his talk "Keep Your Goals to Yourself," entrepreneur Derek Sivers argues that it's better to keep it a secret.

Why might that be? "Any time you have a goal, there are some steps that need to be done, some work that needs to be done in order to achieve it," Sivers explains. "Ideally, you would not be satisfied until you'd actually done the work. But when you tell someone your goal and they acknowledge it, psychologists have found that it's called a 'social reality.' The mind is kind of tricked into feeling that it's already done. And then because you've felt that satisfaction, you're less motivated to do the actual hard work necessary."

It sounds like a bizarre theory. But psychological tests across almost a hundred years—from the 1920s to the twenty-first century—confirm that people who talk about their ambitions really are less likely to achieve them.

So what should we do instead? "Well, you could resist the temptation to announce your goal," suggests Sivers. "You can delay the gratification that the social acknowledgment brings, and you can understand that your mind mistakes the talking for the doing."

And if you really can't bear to keep quiet? Sivers suggests you might at least state your plans in a way that gives you no mental satisfaction. For example, if your goal is to run a marathon, you might say, "I need to train five times a week, and kick my ass if I don't, OK?"

Overall, though, the advice couldn't be clearer. Follow your creative dreams but keep quiet about them. And if you're finding that difficult, then it's all the more motivation to achieve them quickly!

Q FIND OUT MORE

Derek Sivers's talk:
"Keep Your Goals to Yourself"
2010

Also try Tim Ferriss's talk:
"Why You Should Define Your Fears Instead of Your Goals"
2017

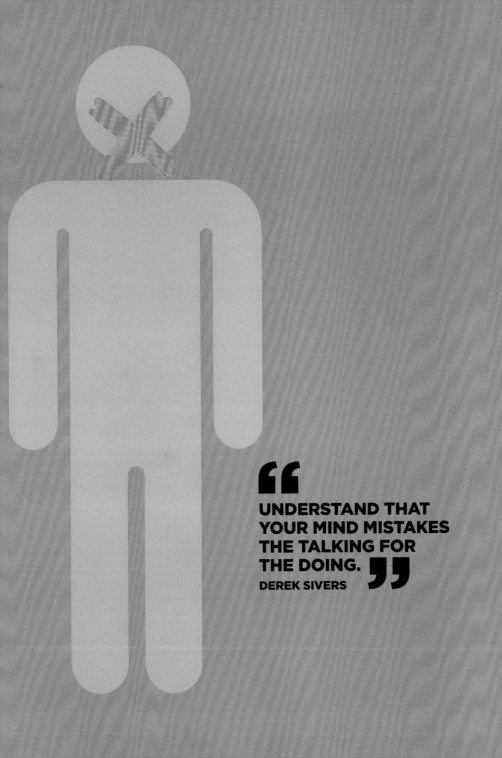

**UNDERSTAND THAT
YOUR MIND MISTAKES
THE TALKING FOR
THE DOING.**
DEREK SIVERS

CAST OFF SELF-LIMITING BELIEFS

Is your mind holding you back? Then reprogram it.

Carrie Green, author and founder of the Female Entrepreneur Association, believes the biggest thing holding us back in our careers is our own mind. In her talk "Programming Your Mind for Success," she argues that "people are missing out on incredible opportunities all of the time, because of what's going on in their head . . . And so these wonderful ideas, and these incredible potentials, stay locked up inside, and you never do anything with them."

This started to happen to her, after she left college to launch her own business unlocking mobile cell phones. "I became more and more negative, more and more self-defeatist, and literally, this positive, optimistic, and go-get person I once was had just disappeared," she reveals. "I'd become totally negative and self-sabotaging. I'd come up with ideas and shoot them down and talk myself out of it."

She realized she would have to "program my mind for success," which is about stepping outside your own thoughts, recognizing them for what they are, taking control of them, and not letting them control you. She took "the negative, rubbish, annoying thoughts and told them to shut up . . . and I replaced them with positive thoughts that were empowering me."

It might sound difficult, and it is. But it worked for Green, and it can work for you. And really, do you have any other choice? Because as Green says, "You just have one life in which to achieve everything you are going to achieve. So you have to act accordingly."

Q FIND OUT MORE

Carrie Green's talk:
"Programming Your Mind for Success"
2014

Also try Alison Ledgerwood's talk:
"A Simple Trick to Improve Positive Thinking"
2013

"I REPLACED THE NEGATIVE, RUBBISH, ANNOYING THOUGHTS AND TOLD THEM TO SHUT UP."

CARRIE GREEN

CROWDSOURCE YOUR WAY TO SUCCESS

Harness the collective intelligence of others.

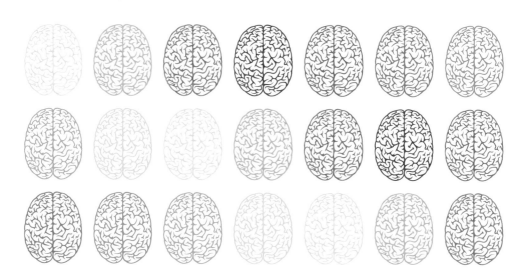

In the twenty-first century, success doesn't need to be something you achieve alone.

Online crowdsourcing enables you to enlist others to help too—many others.

Author and former Microsoft vice-president Lior Zoref did just that, crowdsourcing his talk "Mindsharing, the Art of Crowdsourcing Everything." In it, he describes others who've also benefited from the practice.

For example, pastor Kai Busman puts together his Sunday sermons based on crowdsourced suggestions. Francine, who is raising her son using crowd wisdom on a daily basis, feels as if Supernanny is helping her. And then there's Deborah, whose son had a fever and rash. Within one hour of posting a photo on Facebook, three people warned her he might have Kawasaki disease, and that knowledge may well have saved his life.

Successful crowdsourcing requires just a few things, Zoref explains. "First of all you need a really big crowd. How big? It depends. For example, if you have 300 Facebook friends and they are really engaged, it might work. But if you have 3,000 friends and they are not engaged, it won't."

> ## IF YOU HAVE 300 FACEBOOK FRIENDS AND THEY ARE REALLY ENGAGED, IT MIGHT WORK. BUT IF YOU HAVE 3,000 FRIENDS AND THEY ARE NOT ENGAGED, IT WON'T.
>
> **LIOR ZOREF**

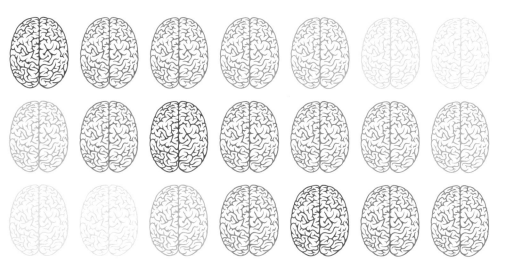

You also need to develop a healthy digital relationship with your audience, he advises. "For example, if you only ask questions, no one will want to be your friend. You need to give value, listen, be responsive, and let them know you value their opinion."

And once you're on board with crowdsourcing, the sky's the limit. To learn about taking things to the next level, check out Luis von Ahn's "Massive-scale Online Collaboration" talk (see page 100).

🔍 FIND OUT MORE

Lior Zoref's talk:
"Mindsharing, the Art of Crowdsourcing Everything"
2016

Also try Aaron Koblin's talk:
"Visualizing Ourselves . . . with Crowdsourced Data"
2011

BE ENERGIZED and develop a daily practice

Finding success in your creative field is one thing; sustaining it is another. This chapter looks at a range of strategies for maintaining your creative energies and developing your skills.

WHY FIRST DRAFTS DON'T NEED TO BE GREAT

First attempts are usually awful, no matter how talented you are.

Do you beat yourself up when your first attempt turns out to be terrible? Well, don't, because even the world's most successful creatives go through the same thing on a regular basis.

Novelist Anne Lamott is among them, as she explains in her talk "12 Truths I Learned from Life and Writing." But the important thing, she says, is not whether your first draft is any good, but whether or not you keep going.

"Every writer you know writes really terrible first drafts, but they keep their butt in the chair," says Lamott. "That's probably the main difference between you and them. They just do it . . . They tell stories that come through them one day at a time, little by little."

The important thing, then, is quite simply to begin, and then keep going. Lamott recalls how, when her older brother was in school, he had a term paper on birds due the following day but hadn't started.

"My dad sat down with him with an Audubon book, paper, pencils, and brads . . . and he said to my brother, 'Just take it bird by bird, buddy. Just read about pelicans and then write about pelicans in

" EVERY WRITER YOU KNOW WRITES REALLY TERRIBLE FIRST DRAFTS, BUT THEY KEEP THEIR BUTT IN THE CHAIR. "

ANNE LAMOTT

your own voice. And then find out about chickadees, and tell us about them in your own voice. And then geese.'"

This is a great example of the principle that if you can't face a big problem, break it down into a series of smaller problems so that it becomes more manageable. For example, if that painting seems overwhelming, start with a sketch. If you're struggling to write a song, start with a riff. And if it's not great, don't panic; just keep going until it is.

Q FIND OUT MORE

Anne Lamott's talk:
"12 Truths I Learned from Life and Writing"
2017

Also try Tim Urban's talk:
"Inside the Mind of a Master Procrastinator"
2016

STOP THINKING YOU CAN'T DRAW

Whatever your discipline, drawing can be a useful tool.

Whatever your creative profession, being able to draw is a useful skill to have. If you're a web designer or an advertising executive, for example, being able to sketch out your ideas for a client is a great way to get a speedy sign-off. Or, if you're a film director or TV producer, you can share your vision with your team through storyboarding. The same idea applies in lots of different contexts.

Unfortunately, many people believe they simply can't draw and so never try. But communications expert Graham Shaw believes that's a mistake. In his talk "Why People Believe They Can't Draw," he demonstrates how mastering a few simple techniques is all you need to be able to draw—but only as long as you also make important adjustments to your attitude.

All young children believe they can draw, Shaw notes, but for some reason by the time they reach fifteen or sixteen, that belief has often left them. With a little bit of practice, though, we can regain that confidence in our drawing abilities. And that has the happy effect of boosting our confidence overall.

After all, if we've been wrong all this time about not being able to draw, Shaw reasons, "How many other beliefs and limiting thoughts do we all carry around with us every day? Beliefs that we could perhaps potentially challenge and think differently about. If we did challenge those beliefs and think differently about them . . . what else would be possible for us all?"

Q FIND OUT MORE

Graham Shaw's talk:
"Why People Believe They Can't Draw"
2015

Also try Graham Shaw's talk:
"How to Draw to Remember More"
2016

HOW TO TELL STORIES

Use the strategies of storytelling to frame your creative narrative.

Whatever your discipline, all creative work is ultimately about storytelling. Hence, Pixar filmmaker Andrew Stanton is a great man to get advice from.

In his talk, "The Clues to a Great Story," Stanton explains that a narrative shouldn't tell you everything. You need to hold a few details back, because audiences like to do some work themselves.

"We're born problem solvers," he explains. "There's a reason that we're all attracted to an infant or a puppy . . . They can't completely express what they're thinking and what their intentions are. And it's like a magnet. We can't stop ourselves from wanting to complete the sentence and fill it in." A good story therefore needs to give people different pieces of information they can put together, like a jigsaw.

Also, your characters need to have a goal they're striving for. "Wall-E's was to find the beauty. Marlin's, the father in *Finding Nemo*, was to prevent harm. And Woody's was to do what was best for his child."

Then there's what playwright William Archer called "anticipation mingled with uncertainty." Stanton explains: "In the short term, have you made me want to know what will happen next? But more importantly, have you made me want to know how it will all conclude in the long term?"

These principles work for all kinds of storytelling, including ad campaigns, website narratives, social media posts, and beyond. By harnessing them to help finesse your craft, your work will soon become more compelling to audiences.

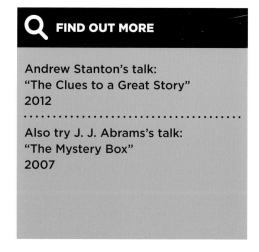

🔍 FIND OUT MORE

Andrew Stanton's talk:
"The Clues to a Great Story"
2012

Also try J. J. Abrams's talk:
"The Mystery Box"
2007

HOW MANY OTHER BELIEFS AND LIMITING THOUGHTS DO WE ALL CARRY AROUND WITH US EVERY DAY?

GRAHAM SHAW

HOW TO BECOME GREAT AT WHAT YOU DO

Practice makes perfect. But how do you get past square one?

We all know that practice makes perfect. But how do you get past the feeling that you're never going to master a skill?

Cirque du Soleil acrobat Avi Pryntz-Nadworny has experienced that very problem. In his talk "The Joy of Practice (Advice from a Circus Performer)," he admits, "We all know with intentional, consistent practice we can accomplish amazing things, but sometimes it seems so far away. Often when I'm practicing or training something, I'll feel like I'm starting from square one."

So how do you get past that feeling that it's all futile? Pryntz-Nadworny suggests you think back to all the other massively complex tasks you've learned in the past that seemed overwhelming at first, but now are second nature. Like, say, riding a bicycle, driving, or typing.

"It's important to remind ourselves that we've accomplished so much in our lives so far," he says. "Take a moment to marvel at the fact that you can type an email without looking down to find each key

before you press it. Or that most of you got here by car today, not giving a second thought to the intricate skills required to get here safely in one piece. These are mind-blowing things that we take for granted on a daily basis."

When you think of it like that, you realize that whether you want to whirl around in a Cyr wheel, juggle fire, or learn any other kind of creative skill, it probably won't be impossible after all.

🔍 FIND OUT MORE

Avi Pryntz-Nadworny's talk: "The Joy of Practice (Advice from a Circus Performer)" 2018

. . . .

Also try Annie Bosler and Don Greene's talk: "How to Practice Effectively . . . for Just about Anything" 2017

TURN ADVERSITY TO YOUR ADVANTAGE

Evolve your creativity by facing new challenges head-on.

Radio host Julie Burstein interviews creative people for a living. In her talk "4 Lessons in Creativity," she reveals that whether she's speaking to a musician, a filmmaker, or a novelist, she often hears the same themes cropping up.

As an example, she says, "Artists [often] speak about how pushing up against the limits of what they can do, sometimes pushing into what they can't do, helps them focus on finding their own voice." She uses the example of Pulitzer Prize–winning novelist Richard Ford, who is dyslexic.

You might imagine that, for a novelist, dyslexia could only be a negative thing. Instead, though, Ford says, "There were a lot of benefits to being dyslexic for me. Because when I finally did reconcile myself to how slow I was going to have to do it, then I think I came very slowly into an appreciation of all of those qualities of language and of sentences that are not just the cognitive aspects of language: the syncopations, the sounds of words, what words look like, where paragraphs break, where lines break."

All of us will face challenges, both big and small, in our work. But what matters is how we respond to them. Do we get stressed and feel defeated when things don't exactly go our way? Or do we, like Ford, turn a positive into a negative, and find our true creative voice in the process?

Q FIND OUT MORE

Julie Burstein's talk:
"4 Lessons in Creativity"
2012

Also try Caroline Casey's talk:
"Looking Past Limits"
2011

HARNESS YOUR HERITAGE

Your background can be a great source of inspiration.

As we discovered in Derek Sivers's talk "Weird, or Just Different?" (see page 39), we can all benefit from learning from other cultures. But it can be even more inspirational to draw on your own personal background and family lineage. Filmmaker and musician Kayla Briët, who grew up in Southern California, does exactly that, creating work that draws on the stories of her Dutch-Indonesian, Chinese, and Native American heritage.

In her talk "Why Do I Make Art? To Build Time Capsules for My Heritage," Briët says that she's always been obsessed with time capsules. "They take on many forms," she explains, "but the common thread is that they're uncontrollably fascinating to us as human beings, because they're portals to a memory, and they hold the important power of keeping stories alive. As a filmmaker and composer, it's been my journey to find my voice, reclaim the stories of my heritage and the past, and infuse them into music and film time capsules to share."

Briët is driven in part by a fear that these cultures might otherwise one day be forgotten. "It can become incredibly dangerous when our stories are rewritten or ignored," she argues, "because when we are denied identity, we become invisible."

Everyone's family tree—whether it's linear or combines a mixed heritage like Briët's—tells a series of fascinating stories, as does the community we grew up in, as Sting explains on page 45. Could yours be the inspiration you need for your next creative project?

Q FIND OUT MORE

Kayla Briët's talk:
"Why Do I Make Art? To Build Time Capsules for My Heritage"
2017

Also try Amelia Laytham's talk:
"Rediscovering Heritage Through Dance"
2016

> **IT'S BEEN MY JOURNEY TO FIND MY VOICE, RECLAIM THE STORIES OF MY HERITAGE AND THE PAST, AND INFUSE THEM INTO MUSIC AND FILM.**
> **KAYLA BRIËT**

LAUNCH A SIDE HUSTLE

You don't have to leave your job to start a creative business.

Many of us would love to start a business, but it's not practical to leave our jobs right now. No problem, says podcaster and marketer Nicaila Matthews Okome in her talk "This Is the Side Hustle Revolution"—just launch one in your spare time.

On her podcast "Side Hustle Pro," Okome has interviewed more than a hundred women who've launched a side project, aka a side hustle. To take two examples, "Nailah Ellis-Brown started Ellis Island Tea out of her trunk. Arsha Jones started her famous Capital City Co Mambo Sauce with one product and a PayPal link."

What Okome has learned is that it's often best to start small. "The goal here isn't necessarily to be the next Coca-Cola or Google," she explains. "Scale is great, but there's also beauty in a successful business that's built for a specific audience."

And even if it doesn't turn out to be profitable, a side hustle is still worth doing.

"It's still an investment in yourself," Okome stresses. "Forty-one percent of millennials who have a side hustle say they've shared this information with their employers. They're not worried about their managers reacting negatively. They recognize all the learning and growth that comes with running a side hustle."

In short, everyone is doing it. So why aren't you? As Okome says, "Side hustles are about embracing that hope that we can be the ones making the decisions in how we spend our work lives."

Q FIND OUT MORE

Nicaila Matthews Okome's talk: "This Is the Side Hustle Revolution" 2019

Also try Liz Navarro's talk: "Millennial Women Are Dominating the Side Hustle" 2017

HOW HUMOR MAKES YOU MORE CREATIVE

A sense of fun can be key to your success.

If you watch some of the more highbrow discussions of the arts on PBS or the BBC, you might assume worlds like painting, sculpture, writing, and classical music are overly serious places, in which people's brows are continually furrowed.

Yet as we learned in Shea Hembrey's talk "How I Became 100 Artists" (see page 48), there's a long tradition of creative parody in the arts. New Zealander comedian, director, and Oscar nominee Taika Waititi explains why he believes that bringing a sense of fun into our work is vital.

In his hilarious talk "Why Humor Is Key to Creativity," Waititi runs through a potted history of his creative career, from his background in painting and visual art to early attempts at filmmaking, illustration work, and even animation.

"I wanted to try every single thing," he stresses. "I come from a background where people have said, 'You have to have one job and stick with it.' Well, I don't believe that. I think that in this day and age, people have things that they want to express, and you need to have a wide range of tools. And filmmaking, painting, acting, poetry, all that stuff, they're all tools."

Most importantly, Waititi believes, you also need to keep a sense of humor about you. "If I can try and make it fun, then that for me is what being creative is about," he stresses. "It's having fun and looking at life through the lens of a child." Shouldn't we all be doing the same?

🔍 FIND OUT MORE

Taika Waititi's talk:
"Why Humor Is Key to Creativity"
2010
. . . .
Also try Ze Frank's talk:
"Nerdcore Comedy"
2004

SLOW DOWN AND FEEL THE BENEFIT

Work at a calmer pace and you'll become more creative.

Our world is getting faster and faster, and it's undeniable that this is having an adverse effect on our creativity, productivity, and happiness.

"We used to dial; now we speed dial," writer Carl Honoré points out in his talk "In Praise of Slowness." "We used to read; now we speed-read. We used to walk; now we speed walk." Yet all this fast living can lead to illness, burnout, and relationship breakdown. So how do we learn to slow down and start enjoying life again?

The secret, Honoré believes, lies in making practical changes to your day-to-day life, such as "taking the time to eat a meal with your family, with the TV switched off. Or taking the time to look at a problem from all angles in the office to make the best decision at work. Or even simply just taking the time to slow down and savor your life."

Self-confessed "rush-aholic" Honoré has done just that. "And the upshot of all of that is that I actually feel a lot happier, healthier, more productive than I ever have," he says. "I feel like I'm living my life rather than actually just racing through it."

It took Leonardo da Vinci several years to paint the *Mona Lisa*, and no one said that wasn't worth the wait. What could you achieve if you make a conscious decision to slow down? And once you've mastered that, maybe it's also time to explore stillness and mindfulness—see Pico Iyer's talk "The Art of Stillness" (page 86) and Andy Puddicombe's talk "All It Takes Is 10 Mindful Minutes" (page 88).

FIND OUT MORE

Carl Honoré's talk:
"In Praise of Slowness"
2005

Also try Matthieu Ricard's talk:
"The Habits of Happiness"
2004

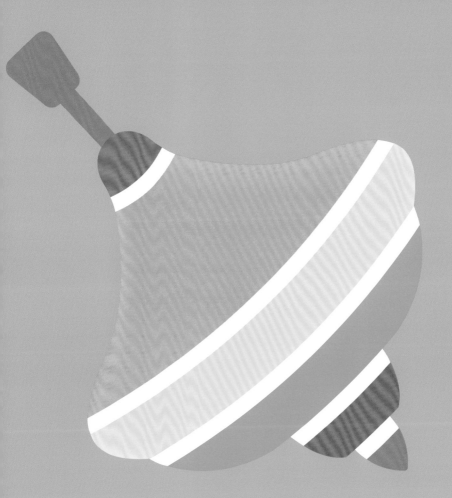

I FEEL LIKE I'M LIVING MY LIFE RATHER THAN ACTUALLY JUST RACING THROUGH IT.

CARL HONORÉ

ASK FOR HELP EFFECTIVELY

You don't have to do it all alone.

Whether you're looking for a mentor, a partner, or just constructive feedback on your work, it pays to ask others for help. But how can you do so effectively? In her talk "How to Ask for Help—and Get a 'Yes,'" social psychologist Heidi Grant offers some pointers.

First, be very specific about the help you want and why. That's because people are scared of giving help badly—unless they're sure what you need, they're going to be reluctant to offer it. For example, Grant cites the LinkedIn requests she gets from strangers "who want to do things like 'get together over coffee and connect' or 'pick your brain.'" She invariably ignores these requests because, she says, "When I don't know what it is you want from me, like the kind of help you're hoping that I can provide, I'm not interested. Nobody is."

Second, never offer to pay people for help, because that can quickly sour a relationship. "Helping one another is . . . how we show one another that we care," Grant points out. If you introduce payments into that, though, it makes your relationship feel less personal and more transactional. "Which, ironically, makes people less likely to help you."

Third, "do not ask for help over email or text," says Grant, because "in-person requests for help are thirty times more likely to get a yes." And finally, follow up afterward. That's crucial, Grant believes, because "what is rewarding about helping is knowing that your help landed, that it had impact, that you were effective. If I have no idea how my help affected you, how am I supposed to feel about it?"

These ideas may be simple, but they really do work. Start using them today, and you'll soon find you have more help than you know what to do with.

Q FIND OUT MORE

Heidi Grant's talk:
"How to Ask for Help—and Get a 'Yes'"
2019

Also try Michele L. Sullivan's talk:
"Asking for Help Is a Strength, Not a Weakness"
2016

TURN PANIC INTO A POSITIVE

To find your creative vision, sometimes you have to "lose it."

The cliché of the film director is someone who knows exactly what they want. Yet Shekhar Kapur doesn't quite fit that mold. In his talk "We Are the Stories We Tell Ourselves," he recalls stepping onto the set of *Elizabeth* in utter confusion. "Ultimately, everybody's looking at you, 200 people at seven in the morning . . . saying, 'Hey. What's the first thing? What's going to happen?' And you put yourself into a state of panic where you don't know."

The film's star, Cate Blanchett, asked him what he wanted her to do. "And I say, 'Cate . . . you're a great actor, and I like to give to my actors: why don't you show me what you want to do?' What am I doing? I'm trying to buy time."

Surprisingly, though, Kapur does not see these fevered moments as a negative. In fact, they're a crucial part of his creative process.

"Panic is the great access of creativity because that's the only way to get rid of your mind," he explains. "Get out of it, get it out. And let's go to the universe, because there's something out there that is more truthful than your mind, that is more truthful than your universe."

Like Kapur, actors and musicians often say their pre-stage nerves are a vital part of their process. And perhaps that approach should be applied to other creative professions too. So the next time you feel a sense of rising panic, don't fight it: it could be just the catalyst you need.

> **PANIC IS THE GREAT ACCESS OF CREATIVITY BECAUSE THAT'S THE ONLY WAY TO GET RID OF YOUR MIND.**
> **SHEKHAR KAPUR**

🔍 FIND OUT MORE

Shekhar Kapur's talk:
"We Are the Stories We Tell Ourselves"
2009

Also try Olivia Remes's talk:
"How to Cope with Anxiety"
2017

BE INSPIRED
and look to
the future

As creatives, we are in a unique position to imagine new visions of the future, for both ourselves and the wider world. This chapter offers advice, tips, and ideas for doing so.

NEW WAYS TO THINK ABOUT THE FUTURE

Fresh sources of inspiration can give you better ideas.

Visions of the future typically come from Hollywood, and include clichés like flying cars.

But in her talk "Reimagine the Future," futurist and designer Angela Oguntala says we should expand our thinking beyond our own experiences.

Why not try, for example, reading Caribbean sci-fi? "It's about aliens that rent the bodies of Cubans so they can vacation on Earth," Oguntala explains. "It's about surveillance robots based on Jamaican folklore and Jamaican magic. It's about a Caribbean postapocalyptic world shaped by extreme weather events and climate change."

This kind of story can give us better ideas, Oguntala argues, because it "makes us aware of the fact that how we imagine the future depends on who is doing it. It depends on that person's traditions, their history, their language, their mythology." So she urges us to "read that Filipino science fiction novel. Watch a Nigerian postapocalyptic film. Look for stories that ask 'What if?' from a new perspective."

It's not just about books but everyday life too. Oguntala suggests that "maybe the next time you go on vacation, you don't only go on safari or lay by the beach, but you find your counterpart in that place . . . You're a Danish engineer and you're in Mexico: go to a university, talk to an engineer, ask her what her dreams and nightmares are about the future."

The message is clear. Expand the way you think about the future, and it could also help you create better work in the present.

FIND OUT MORE

Angela Oguntala's talk: "Reimagine the Future" 2016

Also try Daniel Susskind's talk: "3 Myths About the Future of Work (and Why They're Not True)" 2017

"LOOK FOR STORIES THAT ASK 'WHAT IF?' FROM A NEW PERSPECTIVE. "

ANGELA OGUNTALA

EMBRACE YOUR MULTIPOTENTIALITY

You can succeed in many different areas, not just one.

> ## FOLLOW YOUR CURIOSITY DOWN THOSE RABBIT HOLES. EXPLORE YOUR INTERSECTIONS.
> **EMILIE WAPNICK**

Do you hate the idea of doing the same thing for the rest of your life? You're not alone, says writer and artist Emilie Wapnick in her talk, "Why Some of Us Don't Have One True Calling."

As a youngster, Wapnick feared there was something wrong with her, because she couldn't stick to one thing for long. "I worried that I was afraid of commitment, or that I was scattered, or that I was self-sabotaging," she recalls.

She blames this anxiety on society's habit of asking children, "What do you want to be?" The problem is that "while this question inspires kids to dream about what they could be, it does not inspire them to dream about *all* that they could be. In fact, it does just the opposite."

Why? Because when the youngster lists a string of things they'd like to do, says Wapnick, "well-meaning adults will likely chuckle and be like, 'Oh, how cute, but you can't be a violin maker and a psychologist. You have to choose.'"

In reality, however, that's not the case, and she offers two real-world examples. "This is Dr. Bob Childs and he's a luthier [someone who builds or repairs string instruments] and psychotherapist. And this is Amy Ng, a magazine editor turned illustrator, entrepreneur, teacher, and creative director."

Wapnick argues that such people—who she calls "multipotentialites"—are invaluable members of any workplace. "The specialist can dive in deep and implement ideas, while the

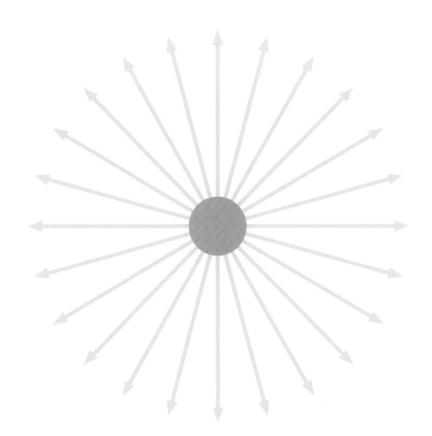

multipotentialite brings a breadth of knowledge to the project," she argues. "It's a beautiful partnership."

As we discovered in Tim Harford's talk "A Powerful Way to Unleash Your Natural Creativity" (see page 13), multitasking actually makes you *more* creative. So if you feel torn between different creative disciplines, don't punish yourself for your instincts—celebrate them! "Embrace your many passions," urges Wapnick. "Follow your curiosity down those rabbit holes. Explore your intersections. Embracing our inner wiring leads to a happier, more authentic life."

Q FIND OUT MORE

Emilie Wapnick's talk:
"Why Some of Us Don't Have One True Calling"
2015

Also try Scott Dinsmore's talk:
"How to Find Work You Love"
2012

FOCUS ON THE DREAM, NOT THE MONEY

Concentrating on the wrong rewards can destroy your creativity.

The idea that people respond to financial incentives seems like a no-brainer. Surely, if you offer people better pay and bigger bonuses, they will work harder and perform better?

According to Dan Pink, previously a speechwriter for Al Gore and now a career analyst, that's not actually the case.

In his talk "The Puzzle of Motivation," he concedes that this approach does still bear results with low-skill, mechanical types of work. But when it comes to creativity and problem-solving, all the research shows that the more financial incentives you offer people, the *worse* their performance becomes.

Why? Simply because for creative people, it's not money that motivates us, but the work itself.

"It's built much more around intrinsic motivation," Pink explains. "Around the desire to do things because they matter, because we like it, they're interesting, or part of something important."

It's time, Pink believes, that we all stopped fighting our instincts and instead embrace them. "If we get past this lazy, dangerous ideology of carrots and sticks," he argues, "we can strengthen our businesses, we can solve a lot of . . . problems, and maybe, maybe, we can change the world."

So the next time you're considering a new project, don't focus on how much it pays; focus on how the work itself will make you feel. Because if it's only the money that excites you, you're unlikely to be happy or productive, or to create anything of lasting value as a result.

Q FIND OUT MORE

Dan Pink's talk:
"The Puzzle of Motivation"
2009
. . . .
Also try Tony Robbins's talk:
"Why We Do What We Do"
2006

FIND NEW WAYS OF GETTING PAID

The internet is providing new financial options for aspiring artists.

We all love the internet, but it's been a financial disaster for many creatives. CD sales have slumped. Piracy has eaten into movie and TV revenue, and newspaper and magazine circulations are in freefall.

But there are two sides to every coin. As musician and entrepreneur Jack Conte points out in his talk "How Artists Can (Finally) Get Paid in the Digital Age," the internet can also offer new ways to earn.

Case in point: Conte and his friend Samuel Yam launched a platform called Patreon, which enables artists of all kinds to be funded directly by their fans. In a way, it's like the historical tradition of the arts being supported by a small number of wealthy patrons, although it's now much more democratic. As Conte explains, "It's going to be different this time because of this; because of the direct connection between the person who makes the thing and the person who likes the thing."

Conte sees Patreon as just one part of a wider network of emerging tools and services that will allow creative people to produce work people love. "Creators are going to come out the other end of this weird hundred years, this century-long journey, with an awesome new machine," he enthuses. "And they're going to be paid, and they're going to be valued."

Have you researched all the different ways you could get paid for your art? If not, then get a move on—you could be missing out on some serious money!

Q FIND OUT MORE

Jack Conte's talk:
"How Artists Can (Finally) Get Paid in the Digital Age"
2017

Also try Hadi Eldebek's talk:
"Why Must Artists Be Poor?"
2016

FILL YOUR DESIGNS WITH JOY

Using the aesthetics of joy can inspire the feeling in your audience too.

As Paul Bennett explained in his talk "Design Is in the Details" (see page 62), design is primarily about solving problems, and we don't usually associate it with the feeling of joy. But maybe we should, suggests designer and blogger Ingrid Fetell Lee in her talk "Where Joy Hides and How to Find It."

Over a decade of inquiry, Lee has discovered that certain things make everyone feel joy, regardless of age, gender, or race. These include "cherry blossoms and bubbles, swimming pools and tree houses, hot-air balloons and googly eyes, and ice cream cones, especially the ones with the sprinkles." And these things all have certain aesthetics in common, such as "round things, pops of bright color, symmetrical shapes, a sense of abundance and multiplicity, a feeling of lightness or elevation."

Perhaps, Lee suggests, if such aesthetics were adopted by more designers, especially those working in architecture and interior design, we would all be more joyous as a result. "Each moment of joy is small," she says, "but over time, they add up to more than the sum of their parts. And so maybe . . . what we should be doing is embracing joy and finding ways to put ourselves in the path of it more often."

Are you struggling to complete a song, a novel, a work of art, or a graphic identity? Maybe the ingredient you're missing is joy. Try adding it, and see what happens.

Q FIND OUT MORE

Ingrid Fetell Lee's talk:
"Where Joy Hides and How to Find It"
2018
. . . .
Also try Stefan Sagmeister's talk:
"Happiness by Design"
2004

HOW TO DESIGN A VISION OF THE FUTURE

When designing for the future, a human-centered approach is most effective.

Designer Anab Jain and her husband spend their time designing visions of the future.

Yet for many of us, the future is happening too fast, causing anxiety and a sense that things are out of control. "And so, we let the future just happen to us," says Jain. "We don't connect with that future 'us.'"

In her talk "Why We Need to Imagine Different Futures," Jain argues that instead, we need to take a more human-centered approach. For example, when she worked with the United Arab Emirates to imagine their future energy strategy, she says, "One of the participants told me, 'I cannot imagine that in the future people will stop driving cars and start using public transport.' And then he said, 'There's no way I can tell my own son to stop driving his car.'"

But the couple were prepared for this. "Working with scientists," Jain explains, "we had created approximate samples of what the air would be like in 2030 if our behavior stays the same. Just one whiff of the noxious polluted air from 2030 brought home the point that no amount of data can."

This is how we can design a better future for humankind, Jain believes. "It means we have the chance to change direction, a chance to have our voices heard, a chance to write ourselves into a future we want." Could this human-centered approach help convince stakeholders that your designs for the future represent the right approach?

🔍 FIND OUT MORE

Anab Jain's talk:
"Why We Need to Imagine Different Futures"
2017

· ·

Also try Dan Gilbert's talk:
"The Psychology of Your Future Self"
2014

CREATE BETTER DESIGNS WITH DATA

Real-time information is making fashion more democratic.

Creatives everywhere are finding new ways to gather customer data and predict new trends. Does that mean the death of true creativity? Fashion buyer Steve Brown argues the opposite: that data is allowing designers to focus more on what they love doing.

In his talk "How Data Is Driving the Future of Fashion," Brown points to the development of smart changing rooms. "[They] have mirrors that are essentially giant touchscreens," he explains. "The mirrors recognize your garments from their tags and let you know: 'Hey, that shirt you're trying on, we have it in these five colors and in these sizes.' And if you want to try on another size, the mirror sends an instant message to the salesperson and voilà, the shirt that you want comes to you."

And that's not all. "Researchers right now have the technology to look up eye reactions of fashion shows," Brown notes. "Just imagine, you're sitting in the front row of a fashion show: your eye reaction could influence the next designer's design."

This doesn't mean designers aren't needed; it just means their role is changing. "I see the future fashion designer as an innovator and a visionary, where the consumer can interact with real-time feedback before anything is made," says Brown. "The designer can design, document, and create within minutes any patterned style or size. They can then 3-D model it and eventually 3-D print it." Could this clever tech help you harness your creativity more fully?

Q FIND OUT MORE

Steve Brown's talk:
"How Data Is Driving the Future of Fashion"
2017

Also try Kaustav Dey's talk:
"How Fashion Helps Us Express Who We Are—and What We Stand For"
2017

DRAW YOUR PERSONAL FUTURE

Visualizing your creative dream will help you achieve it.

Most of us have a creative dream. Unfortunately, says author Patti Dobrowolski in her talk "Draw Your Future—Take Control of Your Life," most of us will never actually pursue it, and that's a shame.

"You can live the life you desire," Dobrowolski believes. "It's right there in front of you. But in order to achieve it, you must first see it, then believe it, and then you must graciously ask and train your brain to help you execute your vision."

The best first step is to visualize your goal, drawing a picture of what you want to happen. As Dobrowolski says, "A picture can create movement. A picture can unite nations, a picture can pull at your heart and fill you with a deep desire to do something."

You don't have to be an artist, or even know how to draw, Dobrowolski stresses. It's more about putting yourself into the right frame of mind to plan your future effectively. "As naive as your drawings might be," she explains, "when you draw where you are, your current state, and where you want to be, your desired new reality, suddenly you have a road map for change."

And then it's just a question of acting on your idea and making it real. "So, every day, you get up, you soak in your picture, you step into the possibility. And this is the most important part: you act on it."

We have only one life. So follow Dobrowolski's advice, and get drawing right now! What do you have to lose?

Q FIND OUT MORE

Patti Dobrowolski's talk:
"Draw Your Future—Take Control of Your Life"
2015

Also try Ashanti Johnson's talk:
"The Power of Visualization"
2018

INDEX OF SPEAKERS AND THEIR TALKS

Unless another website has been stated, the TED talks below can be accessed via the TED website by typing www.ted.com/talks followed by the speaker specific link, for example www.ted.com/talks /tim_brown_on_creativity_and_play.

INDEX

ACKNOWLEDGMENTS

Thanks to Sorrel Wood and Abbie Sharman at The Bright Press, for trusting that a journalist known for writing in short, news-fueled bursts could bring a full book to completion. To my indefatigable project manager, David Price-Goodfellow, who's never anything less than calm under pressure. To my quite brilliant copy editor Susi Bailey, who could spot a typo from the moon and was always full of helpful ways to inject my words with bounce and flow. To designer Tony Seddon, who's been a pillar of strength throughout, and has brought my text to life in magical and inventive ways with his beautiful illustrations. And finally, to the long-suffering love of my life, Julie, whose ideas, suggestions, editing prowess, and tea-making skills have been utterly invaluable to the completion of this book.